THE INNOVATION FACTORY
TAKING THE PLUNGE!

FOREWORD BY YVES PIGNEUR

GILLES GAREL & ELMAR MOCK

CRC Press
Taylor & Francis Group
Boca Raton London New York

CRC Press is an imprint of the
Taylor & Francis Group, an **informa** business

AN AUERBACH BOOK

CRC Press
Taylor & Francis Group
6000 Broken Sound Parkway NW, Suite 300
Boca Raton, FL 33487-2742

First issued in paperback 2022

© 2016 by Taylor & Francis Group, LLC
CRC Press is an imprint of Taylor & Francis Group, an Informa business

No claim to original U.S. Government works

ISBN-13: 978-1-498-74021-0 (hbk)
ISBN-13: 978-1-03-234003-6 (pbk)
DOI: 10.1201/b21329

Dedication

"When everything seems to be going against you, remember that airplanes take off against the wind, not with it."

– Henry Ford

Making breakthrough innovation is no easy matter—it is like teaching a humpback whale to fly or an American eagle to swim. This book is dedicated to all the men and women out there who have taken the plunge!

Contents

Foreword

Isn't it funny how life is full of coincidences. In 2008 I invited Elmar Mock to give a talk on innovation at the University of Lausanne; ever since our paths have crossed regularly. That same year I discovered the C-K Theory of breakthrough innovation that is well known to Gilles Garel, and I wrote an article on its application to research in the field of information systems; ever since, the C-K Theory follows me everywhere in my seminars with PhD students.

I was far from imagining that the creator and the researcher were going to actually meet each other. The former invented the Swatch that would revolutionize the watch industry and then founded Creaholic, an innovation company, organized and run according to rules that are as original as the innovative solutions produced therein. The latter experiments with and spreads the C-K Theory, a theoretical framework and innovation process that explains how to marry ideas, intuition, findings, dreams from time to time, and all of that with a real technical and commercial feasibility of an invention.

When Elmar Mock invented the Swatch, and when he launched Creaholic, he was unaware that he was applying a C-K method of reasoning. When Gilles adopted and spread the C-K Theory, he was unaware that the invention of the Swatch would be one of the most perfect examples of this theory. It was thanks to their meeting one another that they were able to share their thoughts in a harmonious, inventive, and accomplished fashion that will most certainly arouse the curiosity of the reader.

Dear reader, I am convinced you will enjoy discovering the tale, the inside story of the history of the Swatch, along with the thoughts—

sometimes full of imagery, sometimes conceptual—of these two partisans of innovation. It is amusing to read, in the second chapter, the story of the Swatch in light of the C-K Theory. Just as it is amusing to read, in the third chapter, about the C-K Theory finely illustrated by recent examples of innovations designed by Creaholic. The complicity the two authors, masters of innovation, share is tangible.

Throughout all of the chapters we can only be in admiration of the talent of these two partners. The former has a penchant for vibrant metaphors, which help him share his approach, his vision, and his accomplishments with the reader. The molecular metaphor of gas, liquid, crystal in the fourth chapter is a good example of a very intuitive depiction of innovation. The latter is a fervent admirer of the rigor of well-built theoretical constructions, which he passes on to the reader with precision, passion, and a neat sense of examples.

Elmar is not only a creative person he is also an entrepreneur. The organization, the governance of Creaholic, his "innovation kolkhoz," as he describes it himself, are examples of originality in management. In the fifth chapter, the reader will be easily convinced and taken with his rules of managing and astonished by the metaphor of the «matriarch» that Elmar is particularly fond of.

In the last chapter, from the reflection concerning the connected watch, the two authors take pleasure in provoking the reader, inviting him to show some imagination in order to rethink the watch of tomorrow. The underlying message is that the C-K Theory could be a good tool for the channeling of creativity.

Enjoy reading this book. Let yourself be charmed by the great story of the Swatch, the rigor of the C-K Theory, the metaphors of the molecule, and the matriarch and the call to reinvent the watch . . .

– Yves Pigneur
Professor at Lausanne University

About Yves Pigneur

Dr. Pigneur has been a professor at the University of Lausanne since 1984, and has held visiting professorships at Georgia State University, the University of British Columbia, the National University of Singapore, and HEC Montreal. He earned his doctoral degree at the University of Namur, Belgium. Together with Alexander Osterwalder, they authored the international bestseller, *Business Model Generation: A Handbook for Visionaries, Game Changers, and Challenges*, translated into 35 languages. In 2014, they co-authored the new book, *Value Proposition Design: How to Create Products and Services Customers Want (Strategyzer)*. They have been ranked #15 on the *Thinkers50* list of all business thinkers worldwide, and they won its "Strategy Award" in 2014.

Preface

Over the last few years, the words "innovation" and "creativity" have become very popular terms in almost every field. A lot of people use these words, but do they really understand what breakthrough innovation is all about? Do they have the tools, the know-how to actually make it happen?

This book explains how you make breakthrough innovation happen and shows you how to structure a company around it. Indeed, a lot of readers are eager to find out how an Innovation Factory is managed, and they are curious as to how you go about keeping the creative people in the company. If you solve that problem, you can make breakthrough innovation happen faster and more often. In this book, we describe the process of innovation, which is not as complicated as you might think.

This book was written for all the men and women who realize that it is time to take a risk, to take the plunge—for all the managers, the bosses, the students, and for anyone out there concerned about what will happen tomorrow . . . for all those who do not want the future to be merely a continuation of today. The authors are living proof of how two totally different professional figures can join forces and work on a common project to bring out the best, to create, to innovate. A scholar and an entrepreneur share their vast experience in the fields of management, entrepreneurship, and innovation. This sharing of knowledge, in the same vein as biomimetics, increases the knowledge base. Indeed, the art of innovation is multicultural and needs cross-fertilization in order to grow, as will be demonstrated with the telling of the hidden side to the story of the invention of the Swatch in Chapter 2.

The authors have defined as one of their main aims the simplification of the concepts and the terms, such as the C-K (Concept-Knowledge)

Theory. The Swiss entrepreneur and the French professor share between them 70 years of day-to-day experience and offer a European vision of innovation that will be able to complement and hopefully add on to the North American one.

Innovation is not just a case of acquiring aptitude. It is also a question of attitude: Innovators strive to remain creative and active. Therefore, the overall approach of this book is essentially one of action. The example of Creaholic, a successful Swiss Innovation Factory with a team of thirty professional inventors, created in 1986, helps the reader grasp what breakthrough innovation is all about. Thanks to the use of metaphors, the ideas and concepts come across as more persuasive and memorable.

This book has managed to bring together an experienced scholar and a serial entrepreneur who share the same passion for understanding processes and the theories needed to innovate over and over again. The Professor and the Inventor have teamed up to share their skills, their know-how, with anyone who has an interest in the fine art of breakthrough innovation.

Acknowledgments

This book would not have been possible without our innovative friends Ernst Thomke, the father of the Swatch, Franz Sprecher, the man behind the marketing, and Lucien Trueb, a respected watch expert and journalist. They contributed to the historical side of the book. A number of close colleagues have made comments that have influenced this book: Marcel Aeschlimann, André Klopfenstein, and Christoph Berger of Creaholic (The Innovation Factory in Biel, Switzerland). We are also grateful to Mario Tronza and Guy Luttinger (Creaholic) for their illustrations, to Graham Allen (USA) for his stunning cover design, and to Professor Yves Pigneur, a true *connaisseur* of breakthrough business models, who kindly agreed to write the Foreword. It is with gratitude to the team of *"Centre de gestion scientifique"* of *MINES ParisTech* in France, especially Professors Armand Hatchuel, Pascal Le Masson, and Benoît Weil, that we were able to structure our own way of thinking. Of course, certain mistakes remain and are the sole responsibility of the authors.

Finally, we would like to express our gratitude to our families, especially Isabelle and Hélène (muse of the innovator and translator of the original version in French), and to Marje Pollack (DerryField Publishing Services) who provided a careful, conscientious, and intelligent copyedit.

– Gilles Garel and Elmar Mock, October 2015

About the Authors

How do professional innovators work? How do concepts and knowledge influence each other in the Innovation Factory? How do designers think? How does a professional inventor organize his work? This book answers these questions and takes a look at some practical cases: For the first time, you will discover the unknown story of the Swatch watch told by one of the two inventors. Even though it is difficult to make breakthrough innovation and even more difficult to repeat it, we are all potential innovators. This book is an opportunity for the authors to share their knowledge of the fine art of breakthrough innovation management.

Professor Gilles Garel

Full Chair Professor of Innovation Management at the Conservatoire national des arts et métiers (le Cnam) Professor at l'Ecole polytechnique of Paris, France, former Professor at Ottawa University, Canada. Gilles Garel is a researcher at Cnam with innovative companies.

Elmar Mock

Co-inventor of the famous Swatch watch at the age of twenty-six, Elmar Mock created his own "Innovation Factory" company Creaholic in Bienne, Switzerland, in1986. His name as an inventor appears on more than 150 patent families.

Elmar and Gilles are frequent speakers at conferences and industry events.

Chapter 1

Nobody Goes Truffle Hunting on the Highway

This book is the result of an encounter between a serial inventor, prominent in the world of innovation, and a scholar who has been transforming innovative projects for the last 30 years. Elmar Mock is the co-inventor of the Swatch watch and an innovator and founding partner of Creaholic, in Bienne, Switzerland (see Chapter 5). Gilles Garel is a professor at the Conservatoire national des arts et métiers and at the Ecole polytechnique in Paris. What they have in common is a passion for innovation with a need to understand and the desire to make the process of disruptive creativity accessible to all. Elmar Mock took the risk of deciding to go off the beaten track.

So, how do you go about changing the way you think in order to create new ideas that are considered impossible or even unacceptable? How do you create new objects? Nobody goes hunting for truffles on the highway; you go in search of them along the less-trod paths. If you take the side roads, the ones that nobody ever takes, you will finally end up innovating. This might seem like a very simple statement, but how you actually end up on the right route is somewhat more complicated. How do you learn to get off the streets of conformity? Of course, innovation cannot merely be reduced to the art of truffle hunting, or the digging up of gold nuggets. The side roads are a place for conception, for implantation, and for the invention of new objects, in the same vein as unknown varieties of truffles. When innovation hits the market, how do you build a new highway that allows you to go faster than everybody else, keeping ahead by continuously innovating? When several companies are on the same track you have to go faster than your rivals. This is the reason why you have to continue innovating, and radically, for it is not enough to pedal fast to win a stage of the Tour de France—that will only allow you to stay in the pack.

1.1 The Innovator Stops You from Going Around in Circles

Even if all rival companies have (or would have) the need to innovate on a permanent basis, many are wary of innovation, as it always involves a certain amount of risk. This risk is not only a financial one but also a philosophical one of sorts because you have to accept a certain amount of the uncertainty as well as the probability that the result will not correspond to the initial plan and everything might end in failure. Faced with these fears, renovation prevails over innovation: Even if a lot of people swear by innovation, the overwhelming majority are in fact looking for renovation. Everyone dreams of revolution, but they work towards evolution.

Strategic management research can explain, through mimicry, the actions of leaders, but without clear points of reference. When the weather is foggy and you have no clue where you are going, you follow the first

Table 1-1 Evolution—Revolution

Evolution	Revolution
Regulated	Innovative
Exploitation	Exploration
Renovation	Innovation
Known	Unknown
Improve	Transform
Know	Revise
Decompose	Enlarge
Incremental	Radical
Routine	Disruptive

people you come across because it is more reassuring to have them lead the way. But does that mean you are on the right path? When everyone follows everyone else, we all end up going round in circles. Fortunately, innovators are there to break those circles. They refuse to accept the situation as it is. They break the rules, move from side to side, shifting everything around, going beyond the framework in order to challenge and set new ones. They choose the side roads and take the risk of starting a revolution (see Table 1-1).

This book positions itself on the revolutionary side of innovation. Indeed, you do not start a revolution the same way you manage renovation. Revolution does not simply follow a routine; employees who work well in evolutionary work cannot suddenly do something revolutionary overnight. However, the message of this book is positive: Anyone can innovate because innovation does not presuppose any exceptional individual qualities and it is basically no great achievement.

1.2 What Is at Stake for Companies with Contemporary Innovation?

History clearly shows that innovation has always existed. Rome reached a level of "perfection of the social, civil and military technique" (Ellul, 1990, p. 27). The Cistercian Abbeys propagated the watermill along with their organized form of collective lifestyle and their division of labor in a network—a "connected" territory (to use a modern phrase). The first real legislation imputing a monopoly of inventions appears in Venice during the Renaissance, an era when the term «designo» was concocted, which, in its strictest and more modern sense, describes a truly structured activity of conception that precedes the production and development phases. It is important to remember that the Industrial Revolution took place two hundred years ago. With history at hand, we can find traces of the origins of today's innovation, which might even persuade us that nothing is really new in contemporary innovation. But even so, innovation is made up of specific and profound properties. We will examine three examples of this in the following section.

First, contemporary innovation is described as being *intensive* (Le Masson, Weil, and Hatchuel, 2006; Benghozi, Charue-Duboc, and Midler, 2000):

– Innovation was localized; now it is being generalized. In the past it related to certain sectors, to techniques, to the market, and to specific traditions in which creators and designers had a place, a status, assets, and approved methods of work. Today, the place of innovation is more abstract: It touches all sectors, and no company can claim to be innovative enough. All things and situations are potentially innovative, but the notion of innovation remains unclear.

– In the past, innovation was rare and painstaking; it now occurs more frequently. It used to trigger the start of corporate stories and introduced infrequent ruptures during long periods of stability, followed by more incremental periods of progress. But today, in a globalized market where any good idea is rapidly copied and where the income generated by these rare innovations of a new regime of competitive projects based on intensive innovation, wherein the supply of good ideas creates its own demand. With this kind of strategy, referred to as "obsolescent," it is vital to be the first on the market with an innovative offer that will relegate the existing one (our own included) and satisfy a volatile demand. All this must be done in advance of the competitors and before the retransformation of the supply. Since the gasoline crisis, the socioeconomic context of the Western world has drastically changed and, henceforth, fuels these strategies. It is no longer about asking the client what he wants, but more about being the first to offer him what he might need. Nevertheless, the market reaction cannot be fully anticipated, for today you have to "pay to see"; hence, the recurrent launching of development and life cycles of many innovative projects that are shrinking. Profits are made on the new products and services, whose very nature refers to the second characteristic.

This second feature depends on the disruption of the *identity* brought about by contemporary innovation. Indeed, intensive innovation creates a recurrent identity crisis of goods and services in many sectors of activity (Le Masson, Hatchuel, and Weil, 2006). The identity of any object corresponds to the properties commonly associated with it by those who use it, those who distribute it, and those who keep it alive. A bottle, a bank, a car, or a hotel, carry notions with them with which we are all familiar, helping us to recognize them instantly when we see them or think about them. What they are is nothing definitive, as all identities can be changed partially and sometimes completely. If traditional competition means innovating according to parametric criteria of performance (quicker, cheaper, smaller, safer)—that is, improving the object within its given identity in many sectors—the very identity of the object has become uncertain. It is constantly changing as a result of the on-going pressure of progressive technologies, with the new set of social values, new regulations, and new *low-cost* competitors. The accessories of the new mobility perfectly illustrate this instability of identity: Information technology colonized the world of telephony and mobile telephony before moving on to cameras, which, in turn, invaded the world of smartphones. Just as the watch had existed as a nomad object since the 15th century, it has only very recently become a walking library. So what is today's function for a watch, a smartphone, a TV? Where is the boundary between food and medicine? Is a free newspaper a newspaper? Is the *Cirque du Soleil* a circus? Is the Boris bike (a shared bike) still a bicycle? Is the Swatch still a watch (like the other ones) when it is mass-produced in Switzerland, in plastic, and for a production cost 60% less than what we know today? Who had the idea of using a kite on water when we know it was meant for use on land? *Kitesurfing* borrows its identity from surfing, from the *funboard*, and from the kite. Let's not forget the iPhone, which on its release in 2007, transformed the established identity of the mobile telephone. Moreover, is it still a phone or more of a newspaper, a bank, a *jukebox*, a boarding pass, or an encyclopedia? *Smartphones* are not only objects to phone with when we are on the move, they have become multifunctional and multitasking gadgets whose uses cannot be completely understood even by the brands that commercialize them. At the end of the day, they leave it up to the independent developers, who coordinate via platforms and rules of design to create the countless numbers of applications.

Today, we all know what a car is, or a watch, a chair, a telephone, or a night in a hotel, and yet groups of designers are already working on the next redefinition of these things. How do you go about handling this activity of innovative design? How do you revise the identity of objects? This redefinition has nothing to do with luck, and one thing is certain: Miracles never happen. The development of innovation depends on the capacity of the company to imagine other hidden properties of the objects, services, and *processes* that surround us now and in the future (Le Masson, Weil, and Hatchuel, 2010). However, few and far between are the companies who have acquired this capacity of imagination because the scientific, technical, and managerial culture of the West is built on the improvement of the identity of objects.

Finally, contemporary innovation has a *collective* and open side to it. No one innovates on his own, nor in a *task force*, but rather in large, collaborative systems of rival companies (e.g., ITRS and semiconductors). Innovation happens between clients and suppliers (Maniak and Midler, 2008), and even between customers and companies. Moreover, the phrase "open innovation" has become more popular over the last few years, helping to enhance these trends (Chesbrough, 2003). For example, IBM is ranked number eight on the list of the world's biggest holders of patents in the biotechnological field. The car industry and the telecom sectors work together on embedded online data processing systems, while certain companies have even invented the job of "knowledge broker" (Hargadon, 2002) in order to inter-relate fields of knowledge that are traditionally separate. The mobility of knowledge has thus increased over the last few decades, such as the development of *open source* software that can be executed by the coordinated work of thousands of programmers on the world platform.

And so, since the manufacturing days back in the 17th century, the company as such has reinvented itself. Facing the challenges that have just been described, it is essential to identify the organization, the thought process, the performance criteria, and the business model that will allow teams of people to design objects with revised identities up until their commercial use on the market.

1.3 From the Notion of Innovation to Actually Making It Happen

If innovation is both the result of the action of innovation and of the action itself, this book clearly takes the action point of view, which is "ongoing" innovation.

Innovation is a new way of creating value (in a very large sense of the word) for clients, consumers, and the entity at the origin of the innovation itself or for the company. The traditional definitions come from the industrial economy world and encompass invention, innovation, and distribution (see Table 1-2).

If we agree with these traditional definitions, then we must also admit that invention precedes innovation. And, therefore, innovation is a result of

> ### Table 1-2 The Classic Definitions of Innovation
>
> **Invention** is an activity of the imagination and the result of technical means, assets, or new services.
>
> **Innovation** is an invention that is transformed into a product or a service and is used on the market or distributed in society. Innovation diffuses and socializes the invention.
>
> **Diffusion** is the process that describes and explains the adoption of the innovation and its acquisition of a large portion of the population.
>
> Many an invention has never been transformed into an innovation because it was never diffused or because it was useless or unsuited to the requirements or incapable of meeting the market's expectations (no business model, hurdles from the onset, lack of resources . . .).

an invention that can be measured, certified, and observed. These definitions allow innovations to be enumerated, but "it must [should] be possible to have a reference to certain conventions . . . of what makes up the 'new and improved' properties considered easy to understand for the salesman and the buyer" (Oslo Manual, 2005, p. 10). This definition of innovation is very practical for econometrists who want to enumerate the existing innovations on the market with the aim of producing macro-economical statistics. Innovation is defined here as *ex post facto*, already present on the market: It is what is considered new on the market. But this book does not just deal with innovation once it is on the market. It shows how innovation gets onto that market. It takes a look at the people and the organizations that innovate. This book examines the activity and the process of innovation, not the exploiting of an innovative proposal. To be successful, innovative activity must involve an interpretation of the downstream constraints (which are not necessarily the market ones). To refer to the activity or the making of innovation, the term "invention," which (such is the case at least in France) conveys a connotation of the Lépine* examination, relegating any inventive activity to a level of technique, whereas innovation includes numerous other dimensions, such as the business model or the design. In the second part of this book, we will, therefore, discuss the term "innovative design," thereby underlying the importance of the analysis of

---

* The Lépine Examination is a famous French examination of inventions, created at the turn of the 20th century.

the activities of the design, which are able to produce disruptive innovation. The management of breakthrough design has been a topic much researched over these past fifteen years; we will create analytical frameworks that result from this research (see C-K Theory).

1.4 The Entrepreneur and the Scholar

As mentioned earlier, this book brought together a conceptual innovator (whose first project was the Swatch) and a scholar who does "grounded theory" research (resulting in a renewed framework of innovative design). The aim is not to hand out magical formulas of how to successfully innovate thanks to a few tools, nor are we here to tell a few success stories without including any form of critical analysis. Pride of place goes to the theoretical part, not out of pure "academic" joy but rather because a certain amount of rigor is needed to examine the questions that will be raised. In order to come to grips with innovation, you need new theoretical frameworks to be able to approach it as a phenomenon before it ends up becoming an activity. Indeed, the themes of this book could not have been analyzed without involving the professional and the academic world.

The analytical framework put forward here is the C-K theory ("C" for concept and "K" for knowledge) and is dealt with at great length in Chapter 3. It was developed in order to design new objects that break away from familiar identities without necessarily promoting expensive, technical, and complex innovations. The C-K theory is a recent and innovative breakthrough in design, but, above all, it is a very practical theory that can structure a way of thinking about design, thereby helping to organize the collective work of breakthrough design. How do you innovate in the dark? How do you innovate when you no longer know what to invent? This theory defines and provides innovators with a strict procedure for breakthrough innovation.

Why choose the C-K theory when there are so many other tools and theories of innovation and design out there? An analytical framework, even if it is very integrative, is favored in this book, and it is the premise that we uphold. In fact, if it weren't for C-K, the authors of this book would never have met: In December 2008, Gilles Garel had the opportunity to present this theoretical framework to Elmar Mock at Creaholic. The theory corresponded to the innovation projects of the company and shed light on 20 years of innovative design—"This scholar is explaining to us how we work!" Because, just like Monsieur Jourdain (in *The Middle Class Gentleman* by Molière), Creaholic puts C-K unconsciously into practice. Basically, the virtue of a management theory is that it can be useful for action by enabling those who "do" but who are probably unable to really explain "how they do it." The management researcher and the practitioner both relate to these "practical theories." In this type of relationship between practical scholar and reflexive practitioner, the former renews and enriches his case base and validates or invalidates his theoretical framework, while the latter finds an overall value in his work and his innovative, unique methodologies. Moreover, together they can conceive new pragmatic theories. Creaholic, as a small disruptive innovation company (see Chapter 5), seeks greater credibility concerning its methodology with its important industrial clients. But which methodology, which product framework, or which breakthrough innovation company will prevail? It will not be the rule-based renovation one. In claiming responsibility for a demanding analytical framework for its activities, the company that innovates for its clients not only clarifies its work processes and its way of thinking, it also undermines the popular management myth that innovators are "young dishevelled guys with beards" or "inventors in your back garage" (Godelier, 2009). To sum up, the adoption of this theory helps professionalize the company image and makes for a better understanding of what professional inventors actually do.

Despite the fact that this book is not purely academic, it should still be taken seriously as it presents proven cases. It is a "practical" book for innovators and innovative organizations that deflates the windbags of innovative managerial self-satisfaction and rejects certain recurrent, hasty explanations of what an innovation factory is—luck, charismatic leaders, vision, courage, and stubbornness. These "innovation engines," well-worn in a certain form of literature and many a management speech, are put aside in favor of a design that strives to be stronger and more well-founded.

1.5 Innovation Was, Is, and Will Be . . .

Like a Chinese soup, simultaneously sweet and sour, this book aims to reconcile in the same process concept with knowledge, imagination with rational thought, a touch of madness with scientific facts, forecast with surprise, anarchy with organization, fizz and chaos on one side, order and logical thinking on the other.

The remaining part of the book will examine the main theme of breakthrough design from two angles. First, we will tell the tale of a very famous innovation whose name is very well known (the Swatch watch), but its story is less so. Secondly, we will highlight the framework of breakthrough design that is the backbone of the whole of the book. Chapter 2 presents the hidden side of the design of the Swatch, because, behind the successful world-renowned brand, the story of how the watch was made is unknown. The role Elmar Mock played and the use of new sources will help retrace the history and explain the principles of an innovative concept, rich in lessons to be learned. The C-K theory will serve to expound on the innovative process and will be described in the ensuing chapter, which will also clarify vocabulary and illustrate methodology with some concrete examples. The fourth chapter chronologically picks up from where we left the innovator who, after having designed the Swatch, went through a difficult patch, a sort of post-innovation baby blues. The company evolved and he felt he could no longer fulfill his creative dreams therein. So he set up his own company. This evolution is the perfect opportunity, in this book, to introduce the molecular metaphor about innovation, which presents three different mental states that help see the interior conflicts and the frustrations of innovators in an environment that rarely understands them. This metaphor sheds light on how difficult it really is to create disruptive innovation and also helps to explain what makes breakthrough innovation possible. Chapter 5 shows how a breakthrough innovation company functions and is managed. How do you organize the work of such a company? What are the rules of governance? This chapter will take a long look at Creaholic and its professional inventors. The book ends with an epilogue and a conclusion. This epilogue is prospective, as it handles the subject of the recent development of connected watches. This topic enhances the main theme of the book of watchmaking design. New entrants, such as Apple or Samsung, have burst into the market with a new object, a watch that is no longer a watch. What is at stake is the redefining of what we will wear on our wrist tomorrow.

Starting with a detailed history of an example of a breakthrough design, along with other examples, this book proposes an analysis that we can all grasp and which gives us a more global view of design theory.

Chapter 2

The Hidden Side of the Concept of the Swatch

The "Swatch" is a quartz (or analogical) watch that is welded in plastic, plain, reliable, very inexpensive to manufacture, and possesses the quality and the durability of traditional Swiss watches. Thanks to the styles, the motifs, and the infinite number of colors that have been created over the years, it is more than just a functional object. It is also an aesthetic and emotional one. The breakthrough design has turned it into a fashion accessory in never-ending renewed collections. For some of us, Swatch is even an object of art, a sought-after collector's item. On March 1, 1983, the first Swatch watch appeared on the Swiss market. Today, "Swatch" is found among the iconic brands of the world. More than 550 million watches have been sold since it was first launched. Before the Swatch, it seemed impossible to mass-produce and sell a Swiss quality watch for barely 50 Swiss francs, while still making comfortable margins. As mentioned before, the story of this watch is seemingly so well known that it seems rather pointless to go back to it. All the same, since the early 1980s, the official story told by the Swatch Group, encouraged by the general management, and reinforced by an overall tendency to analyze the watch from the distribution point of view of the existing product show that the real origins of the Swatch are, in fact, unknown. This period and this story teach us a lot about how you make innovation, and that is where our interest lies.

How was the Swatch invented? Where did the original concept come from? How was the watch developed as a technical object as well as a mass-produced manufacturing process?* What are the innovative management principles that can be learned from its design? This chapter will look back on the major stages of the design of the Swatch between 1980 and 1983—from the materialization of the concept to its launching on the market.

Along with Ernst Thomke, their boss, Elmar Mock and Jacques Müller are the two Swiss-French engineers who are officially recognized as the inventors of the Swatch. On September 16, 2010, they received the prestigious Gaia prize in the category "Creation Craftsmanship" for their invention of the Swatch.† Contrary to the commonly held belief, the famous watch was not invented by Nicolas Hayek, who joined the firm more than two years after its creation (Wegelin, 2009). This chapter ends on a note concerning the paternity of this innovation.

Our intention is neither to restore to favor the key players nor to question the role played by others, nor is it to rewrite history. Indeed we are not historians, and we only had limited access to company archives. "I have decided to reflect on the past, from a non-historian point of view, not in an attempt to rectify the truth. Like a storyteller, I simply want to share an amazing experience in the hopes of helping reveal the subtle and versatile factors which allow innovation to grow and to materialize," explains Elmar Mock. By going back to the concept of the Swatch, new conclusions can be drawn that differ from those that arise out of the analysis of the product's "on-the-market" success: It is important to learn from this concept in order to maintain our capacity to innovate. The lessons learned from the design of the Swatch are still relevant; they are just unknown or simply misunderstood.

The marketing saga of the Swatch would not have been possible without the innovative work of the engineers, and, conversely, the watch would never have known such success without a new concept and a breakthrough design. This book proposes an approach to breakthrough design that is based on both rigorous and continual interactions between concept and knowledge, produced equally by the engineers and the marketing experts.

---

* The word "process" will be used for the process of manufacturing or production, thereby referring to a term commonly used in the sector.
† The press release is cautious—it speaks of "inventors of new technical solutions contained in the patents of the concept of the original Swatch watch."

Thirty years after its creation, the same watch (or almost) is still being made—an exceptional achievement for any electronic consumer product.

At the end of the 1970s, the Swiss watch industry was facing a major crisis that threatened its very existence. The Swatch project turned out to be a marvellous riposte to the economic crisis, and this book retraces the main stages of its development. First, the technical and functional aspects of this conception will be examined from a chronological point of view. Then, the analytical framework of "concept knowledge" will be applied.

2.1 The Great Watch Crisis of the Late 1970s, or When Managers Are No Longer Entrepreneurs

"The Swiss watchmaking industry demonstrated an insolent supremacy towards its British and American rivals in the international fairs organized in the middle of the 20th century" (Donzé, 2009, p. 30). After WWII, Switzerland controlled 90% of the world's watch production and continued to hold 85% up until 1970. In just ten years, its share of the market collapsed, and in 1980 it only controlled 22% of the world's watch market. In 1983, this share of the market dropped even further, to a mere 15%. Asian competitors, mainly Japanese, started pushing the Swiss out, notably by offering cheap quartz watches. The crisis was not limited to the watchmaking sector, but also concerned oil, currency, and social issues. Many Swiss industries that had previously flourished were now threatened with extinction. All over the world Japanese firms dominated the electronic sector with cameras, camcorders, and hi-fi.

2.1.1 The Watch Barons Ensnared by the Models of the Past

At the beginning of the 1980s, the Swiss watch industry seemed condemned to disappear. However, Swiss manufacturers did not react immediately to this collapse, convinced of their technical superiority. They continued to believe that good timepieces could only be mechanical. "The quartz and digital watches are mongrels and have no claims to belonging to the noble family of watchmakers" was what was heard in the sector. The industry was convinced of its domination of the noble art of watchmaking, with a

Table 2-1 The Cartelization of the Swiss Watch Industry

Without going all the way back to Jean Calvin, who prohibited the wearing of jewelry and forced the goldsmiths and jewelers of the middle of the 16th century to develop and innovate in another field—that is, that of watchmaking. It is to be remembered that the economic marasmus that ensued after World War I severely affected the Swiss watch industry. To stand up to the instauration of the customs' protectionist tarifs for the United States, one of the main markets of Switzerland, the sector reorganized itself completely by creating a watch cartel that regrouped on a national level, all of the watch producers. The objective was to install a system of minimum prices among the watchmakers to avoid "chablonnage."[*]

When the watchmaking industry is struck again by crisis in the 1930s, the "cartel" is reinforced by two decisions. First and foremost, the creation of ASUAG in 1931 reinforces the industrial concentration. Afterwards, the Federal government, for once, intervenes (and massively so) in order to save jobs and help the indebted banks. At the end of the 1970s, the two most important companies of the cartel are ASUAG and SSIH.

ASUAG owns the largest watch movement[†] manufacturers: the prestigious Ebauches SA,[‡] as well as brands such as Longines and Rado. For its part, SSIH (founded in 1930) owns the brands Omega, Tissot, and Lanco.[§] These two companies design and produce watch parts and quality watches. Finally, the cartelization brought private interests (the maintaining of numerous family companies constitute the elementary links in the value chain of this industry) together with the interest of the general public (the maintaining of jobs in the Jura area) and has succeeded in improving/cleaning up a fragmented industry, a recurrent victim of the unfavorable climate/situation (Koller 2003).

---

[*] The chablonnage is the exporting of watches in the form of separate parts (complete parts of separate movements) that are mounted in the countries where the watches are sold. The objective is to avoid custom tax on the finished pieces. The Swiss manufacturers were worried that with this "practice," the know-how would be transferred to the foreign workshops that assemble pieces, and that, sooner or later, new rivals would emerge.

[†] A movement is a set of mechanisms used to display units of time. An ébauche is a sum of pieces that are un-assembled of the parts and commercialized in this form.

[‡] Ebauches SA is a very important group of "ébauches" that belongs to ASUAG. ESA lost its corporate identity in 1984 and found itself integrated into the group ETA, also a member of the new group ASUAG-SSIH. In other words, the group of company members of ESA were placed under the control and name ETA.

[§] Lanco is a huge company that produces inexpensive watches at Solothurn.

very genetic and genealogical perception of the subject. "We know how to make watches. We are unique!" The chronometric competitions that rewarded the precision of the watches also helped increase national pride. A foreigner cannot be a watchmaker in Switzerland because the know-how is handed down from generation to generation. "I am the boss, my son will become the boss. We were born to be bosses, and we Swiss know how to make this industry work." Towards the end of the 1970s when the Swatch appeared on the scene, the Swiss watchmaking industry already boasted a secular and prestigious history, having already survived many a crisis largely thanks to the cartel that it had established (see Table 2-1).

2.1.2 Precision Is No Longer a Measure of Quality

Switzerland invented quartz technology, the liquid crystal displays, and the first electronic watches, but the Asian countries were the first to transform these technologies into new products at the end of the 1970s. These countries flooded the world markets with their digital quartz and analogical wristwatches. They replaced the inexpensive, but less accurate, Swiss mechanical watches, like the Roskopf.

From then on, anybody and everybody could make an accurate time-piece without any real skills in the fine art of watchmaking. This represented an upheaval, a major paradigm shift in the sector: the accuracy of watches no longer depended on the quality of the work or on the production cost.* The wristwatch was now available to all, and the Swiss were the big losers in this revolution. Any company could buy the quartz movements at very low prices and enter the world wristwatch market. ASUAG controlled the design and the manufacturing of the mechanical movements through Ebauches SA; it had no more valid reason to exist!

The consequences of the crisis were truly catastrophic for local employment. Between 1970 and 1980, the Swiss watch industry lost two thirds of its workforce, going from 90,000 to roughly 30,000 workers. Of the 300 million watches sold in the world in the early 1970s, only 80 million were produced in Switzerland. Quartz swept aside the "mechanical movements," transforming the Swiss watch industry by turning it into a museum for luxury brands. At the beginning of the 1980s, Switzerland was totally absent from a world market of 450 million watches made for

---

* The cost price of a Swiss watch is based on the time it took to produce quality, high-precision work. The sales price is not determined by the amount of or quality of work that went into the making of a watch, but rather on the image of luxury portrayed by the prestigious brands.

less than $100, while it represented 97% of the market for watches over $350 (Moon, 2004). Foreign competitors even offered to buy up prestigious brands such as Omega, Longines, or Tissot.

2.1.3 The Hayek Report, or the Rapid Concentration within the Sector

In 1980, the Swiss watch industry was doomed to disappear off the face of the earth. Two giants in the sector, SSIH and ASUAG, were on the verge of being abandoned by their banks, which were terrified by their annual losses (amounting to nearly half a billion Swiss francs). ASUAG lost roughly 150 million Swiss francs in 1981–1982, with a very high level of debt (Komar and Planche, 1995, p.18), whereas between 1981 and 1983, the Swiss banks injected more than 900 million francs in ASUAG and SSIH (Donzé, 2009, p.171). In the spring of 1982, the banks employed an external consulting firm—Hayek Engineering, created by N. Hayek twenty years earlier—in order to carry out a study. A few months later, in October 1982, the report, subsequently referred to as the "Hayek Report," presented a certain number of measures that would allow these companies to survive and to bounce back into action. The two main proposals of Hayek, also a consultant for the banks of the watchmaking industry, were the fusion of ASUAG and SSIH and the launching of a new, inexpensive, and good-quality watch (Gabarro and Zehnder, 1994). Indeed, it was this second proposition that would create the myth of him as being the father of the Swatch. In order to avoid the worst-case scenario, the banks and the Confederation sponsored the fusion of ASUAG and SSIH and asked Nicolas Hayek to initiate it on December 8, 1983. The new group was now called *"ASUAG-SSIH, Société Suisse pour l'Industrie horlogère."*

Even though the financial situation improved from 1984 onward, the banks backing the fusion handed over the majority of the capital to a group of private investors directed by N. Hayek. In 1986, *"ASUAG-SSIH Société Suisse pour l'Industrie horlogère"* was renamed *"SMH"* (*Société de microélectronique et d'horlogerie*). N. Hayek bought even more capital at very advantageous rates, and took direct control of the SMH in the same year. He pocketed the Swatch (which had been developed between 1980 and 1983 at ETA, Granges), along with a portfolio of prestigious brands. After the founding of SMH, the name ETA SA included all the companies of the new group that made watch movements. Hayek became the president and administrator designated by the board of administration and CEO of the SMH in 1986. However, during this period and up until 1991, Dr. Ernst Thomke continued to run the company as general director. The company was renamed the Swatch Group in 1998.

Hayek had managed to create a considerable concentration in a single sector that had, for many centuries, managed to conserve small, long-established manufacturers along with their partners, in order to make a profit in terms of industrial streamlining (already underway with the creation of the Swatch), but also in terms of a globalized marketing policy.

2.2 Innovation versus the Crisis: The Empire Strikes Back with the Swatch

The Swatch had never been planned. It was not the result of a deliberate innovation strategy, a carefully thought-out plan, or a brilliant vision. The story of the Swatch started at the end of 1979 at ETA, a key firm in the Swiss cartel owned by Ebauches SA, which in turn was controlled by ASUAG.

Everything began with the unlikely encounter between three people of the ETA firm[*]: a respected senior manager and two young engineers at the bottom of the corporate ladder. The organization of ETA did not *a priori* have the intention of bringing them together (see Table 2-2).

2.2.1 Head in the Cogs

"With Jacques, who had become a close friend, we worked on a lot of projects of development of parts. We had long discussions about the future of watchmaking, trying to imagine what the watch of tomorrow would look

---

[*] As we will find out later on in this chapter, from 1981, marketing and design appeared on the scene of the Swatch project. Other actors made their mark, as well. Brought in as an external consultant, Franz Sprecher will be the decisive man behind the marketing of the Swatch. He invented the name "Swatch" in September 1981. Recommended by Jacques Müller, Bernard Müller and Maryse Schmid are the creators of the final design of the Swatch.

Table 2-2 The Original Protagonists of the Swatch Project

Ernst Thomke was born in 1939. After training as a mechanic at Ebauches SA in Granges, he studied natural sciences and chemistry at the Universities of Bern and Lausanne. He continued his studies at medical school in Bern and then at the INSEAD school of marketing and management at Fontainebleau, France. In 1978, E. Thomke was 39 years old and already had an impressive industrial track record to his name when he was called in to rescue ETA from the crisis. In 1982, he was appointed chairman of ASUAG. He was general manager of SMH from 1984 to 1991, where he took on other industrial challenges. E. Thomke is currently one of the most well-known and well-respected Swiss industrialists, with the reputation of being a "hard" man, not only because of his character but also because of his habit of sacking people.

Elmar Mock was born in 1954 in La Chaux-de-Fonds, hometown to the Musée international de'horlogerie (International Museum of Horology). The son of a watchmaker and engineer in micromechanics from the school of Bienne, Elmar Mock is a qualified watchmaker and micromechanic by training. ETA offered him his first job in 1976, despite the crisis in the sector at that time. Out of the 16 graduates of his engineering school, he was the only one to be hired. Once he joined ETA, E. Mock continued his training as an engineer, in plastics, and this would affect the story of the Swatch.

Jacques Müller was born in 1947 in Porrentruy in the maternity ward of the Hôtel-Dieu, which is now the Musée d'Hôtel-Dieu. He graduated as a micromechanics engineer from St-Imier and was first hired by Ebauches Tavannes, a company specializing in watch movements. There he acquired a good deal of know-how and a good deal of experience in the electromechanical and micromechanical aspects of watchmaking. When Ebauches Tavannes closed in 1978, Jacques Müller joined ETA, where he would work with Elmar Mock.

---

like even though neither of us had been asked to do that!" remembers Elmar Mock. In October 1979, Elmar Mock and Jacques Müller took a course on metal sintering at the University of Esslingen in Germany. They spent most of their spare time together by imagining how to make a very large quantity of watches at a very low cost; it was just mucking around in a bar at this stage," but it turned out that they were in fact imagining the main elements of what would become the Swatch. At that time the two engineers who were working on improving watch parts at ETA had not received any orders concerning any other projects.

Elmar Mock had and still has his "head in the cogs."[*] His passion was tinkering with mini-motors and mechanisms. When he started at ETA in 1976, business was slow. To keep him busy, the director, Fritz Scholl, entrusted him with a plastic injection-molding machine, purchased unofficially and hidden away in an attic in Granges. Why so many secrets? At that time, according to the rules governing the division of labor in the watch industry, ETA was only allowed to make dry-cut brass for the bases of its plates, whereas the other *Ebauches* firm of Fontainemelon only made wet (oil-cut) brass and *Ebauches Electroniques S.A.* in Marin had the monopoly on plastic and was not allowed to work with brass. F. Scholl was aware that polymers would become more and more important in the near future and did not want to be dependent on Marin in order to carry out his experiments. He, therefore, invested in equipment for Mock to work undercover on this personal task. In this way, Mock started his professional career by working "hands on" with plastic without any previous training in the field. Frustrated by his lack of knowledge but nevertheless fascinated by these new materials, he decided, with the approval and the financial support of top management, to go back to college. Mock was sent to Brugg—located in the Swiss-German part of the country—for two semesters. He returned in 1978 with a degree in plastics engineering. He could now pursue his experiments with innovative techniques at ETA, trying to imagine inexpensive and reliable solutions for watchmaking. Still without any specific assignment, he developed and made insulating elements, testing the soldering by ultrasound and imagining new possibilities, thanks to the polymers. This is where the technical design of the Swatch began without anyone actually realizing it.

2.2.2 The Unlikely Encounter

After a few years the small injection-molding machine used by E. Mock in the attic was just not enough. To open up more possibilities of experimentation, he needed more substantial technical means. "I wanted to play . . . I needed a Nestal which cost at that time half a million Swiss francs, but I had no real reason to order one." And that's how, without any specific orders from the hierarchy and just because he wanted one, E. Mock ordered a new-generation plastic injection-molding machine.

---

[*] *Libération*, 13/06/1995.

The internal circuit process forwarded the investment request, which ended up on the desk of Ernst Thomke, General Manager of ETA. On the morning of March 27, 1980, at 11 a.m., Mock was summoned by Dr. Thomke's secretary to a 1 p.m. meeting. "Oh damn!" thought Elmar. "It's about the machine." In the space of two hours, he had to come up with some convincing arguments to justify the purchase! Thomke would most certainly sack him if his only argument was the need to satisfy his personal creative curiosity. He rushed into the office of his friend Jacques Müller, and, at that precise moment in time, their lives and the history of Swiss watchmaking changed forever. . . .

The two men somehow managed to transform the risk into an opportunity and decided to show a sketch of a plastic quartz watch to Ernst Thomke in an attempt to justify the purchase of the machine. They used some of the ideas that they had hatched during their unending philosophical–technical discussions at the University of Esslingen. In less than two hours, Mock and Müller hastily scribbled on graph paper the sketch of the watch that such a machine would be able to produce, coloring it in pink and blue. The drawing was simple, almost childlike. "As we were pressed for time, Jacques and I came up with a design that already included the essential elements of the future Swatch." This was the *"Schnaps-Idee"* (a Swiss-German term for an idea born from bar room banter), the technical brief of what they had in mind. The technical concept of the future Swatch was already there: a single-piece case, welded glass, and a separately mounted motor. The future watch was dubbed Vulgaris.[*] A fearful E. Mock walked into Ernst Thomke's office. His job and that of Jacques was on the line. "What is the use of such a machine? Do you just want to play with it!?" Thomke was reputed as sometimes having violent reactions. "He told me straight to my face that I was unrealistic, irresponsible, and immature. I was in such a state and felt ashamed of myself," remembers Elmar Mock. After having been his punching bag for roughly 30 minutes, Mr. Thomke stopped shouting and asked me, "What do you want to do with this machine?" Elmar Mock took out of his satchel a childlike drawing—the sketch of the Vulgaris[†] (see Figure 2-1). "We could make watches like that!"

---

[*] Later on, the watch was renamed Popularis, then Calibre 500, and, finally, Swatch.

[†] J. Müller drew the sketch.

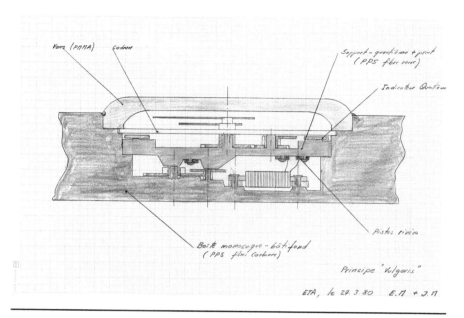

Figure 2-1   The first drawing of the Vulgaris, the future Swatch: Elmar Mock and Jacques Müller (March 27, 1980). (*Source:* Drawn by J. Müller.)

Ernst Thomke responded at once: "I've been waiting for this over a year now! Can I hold onto that piece of paper?" What Mock and Müller did not know at that time was that Thomke had already asked R&D of ETA for designs of low-end watches, but to no avail (see Table 2-3). Upon laying his eyes on the Vulgaris drawing, he recognized the significance of the concept and the choice of a simplified structure. He was quite familiar with watch mechanisms and saw in the design an innovative product and a potential process. He realized it would be possible to win back some of the ground the firm had lost at the lower end of the market by offering a viable alternative to Asian electronic watches and yet without competing with the existing Swiss offer.

2.3 The Swatch Project Did Not Simply Appear Out of the Blue

Without realizing it, each of the three men had been working on the same project. On the one hand, Ernst Thomke, along with senior managers of ETA, had already been thinking about a watch that would be able to

Table 2-3 Swatch and Delirium: A Suspicious Liaison

With the Delirium Tremens, the innovative image of the Swiss watch industry was greatly enhanced, even if the watch was not a commercial success. The Delirium was a technological challenge taken up by ETA, which succeeded in commercializing the thinnest watch in the world, with its mere 2mm. Immediately afterwards, P. Renggli, chairman of ASUAG, ordered ETA to imagine an inexpensive, mass-produced watch (a sector at that time that had been put aside). The company's' survival was at stake. "[O]ften it is said that the Swatch was born out of the Delirium Tremens, the famous gold watch, the thinnest watch in the world, launched in January 1979. The history of the Swatch has therefore theoretically, a pre-history. During 1979, the management of ETA tried on many occasions to define the essence of a new product that came out of the Delirium. This type of research and project was baptised under the code Delirium Vulgaris. All sorts of possibilities are analyzed, the liquid crystal display concept or the analogical Roskopf style, without anything being definitely or clearly accepted."* It was during the autumn of 1979 that E. Thomke, in this same context, wrote the technical brief of a new watch to be developed, a simple but structured list of requirements (cf. infra). R. Carrera (1991, p. 20) wrote that "there were no approaches from the technical management level of Ebauches SA to produce a Delirium type watch in plastic" and that in any case the ressemblance of the Delirium Tremens with the Swatch "stops there as does the comparison between a plane and a goldfish: possessing a similar general form of fuselage" (Ibid., p. 17). And so the architecture of these two watches is quite different, contrary to the belief of the partisans of a filiation. The Swatch is a simplified redesign of the watch, whereas the Delirium Tremens shifts traditional parts of a watch around towards the edge in order to flatten them.

---

* This quotation, presented as an excerpt from *Swatchissimo* by R. Carrera on the worldtempus website (official website of famous brands of watches), is not in the original edition (http://www.worldtempus.com/fr/encyclopédie/index-encyclopédique/histoire-de-lhorlogerie/le-phenomene-swatch/lextraordinaire-aventure-swatch/la-genese/).

compete on the market at the end of 1979, launching various projects at that time.* On the other hand, Mock and Müller imagined, drew, and started to test technical solutions for an industrial combat watch.

---

* The book *Swatchissimo* (Carrera 1991, p. 16), which we recommend to the reader, goes to great lengths to explain the project Delirium Vulgaris and the meetings and discussions that ensued with the managers of ETA of the time, such as A. Bally, A. Begner, U. Giger, or P. Renggli (the Chairman of ASUAG).

Thomke was looking for something that was to be finally invented by Mock and Müller. This encounter between someone "official" who was searching for something and someone "unofficial" who had found something was crucial.

Thomke reacted all the more quickly because he was already involved in an innovation process, even though he had not found anything as of yet. He immediately placed his trust in Mock and Müller, adopting the new idea and offering them his unwavering support. By taking such a risk and circumventing traditional managerial practices, Thomke became the true entrepreneur of the Swatch. The involvement of this brilliant, feared manager along with the industrial power of the ETA Company was what was needed for the Swatch to see the light of day (Table 2-3).

After his meeting with E. Thomke, E. Mock went back to his workplace plagued with doubt and tried to explain to J. Müller how badly the meeting had gone. Both were convinced they would be among the next group of people to be made redundant at ETA. "I went home very sheepishly, repeating to myself that I had made a huge mistake," admitted E. Mock. Urs Giger, head of the technical Department at ETA, shouted at both of the two engineers: "You went to see Mr. Thomke with this strange un-technical piece of paper that represents a project that nobody knows anything about? Have you gone crazy? There is no project, no number! What are you playing at? They want all the plans in six months!" The support of Thomke was unconditional, but it was only going to be granted for a short period of time: Mock and Müller would have very little time to prove what they were capable of.

2.3.1 When the Watch Is the Best Way of Diversifying Watchmaking

The project was launched immediately, without any business plan, no technical brief, no cost study, no market survey,* and without any calculation

---

* Franz Sprecher, the marketing man of the Swatch, explained that "if we had questioned people, they would have *a priori* considered that a plastic watch could not be of good quality"; on the other hand, as we will see later on, the marketing process would offer a new vision based on the technical knowledge of engineering.

of return on investment. It was the crude drawing that E. Thomke used to define the main orientations (open space) and constraints (closed space) of the process:

— The manufacturing cost of the watch had to be less than 10 Swiss francs.
— It would serve as an industrial combat watch (i.e., reconquering of lost ground).
— It had to be mass-produced in Switzerland—a "Swiss-made" watch.
— How does it work? Like a watch!
— What sort of hands does it have? Like a watch!
— How do you set time? Like a watch!

This list of technical requirements was written before the meeting between Mock and Thomke, an indirect consequence of the launching of the Delirium Tremens (see Table 2-3). It is precisely because E. Thomke had already thought about a new watch that he understood the impact of the Mock Müller proposal. If you want to diversify watchmaking, you have to make watches; it's as simple as that! This apparently simple and commonplace idea was absolutely revolutionary! The Swiss watchmaking industry was really stuck in a rut, obsessed with the need to improve on what was already mastered—the grand art of mechanical watchmaking. For E. Thomke, the best diversification of the watchmaking world was the watch itself; it was necessary to design a watch that was similar to others but which possessed new features and (therefore) at a very low cost. These revolutionary properties had to be invented. They had nothing to do with Asian know-how or with traditional Swiss watchmaking *savoir-faire.*

In 1980, the price of the cheapest quartz movement on the market was 14 Swiss francs. The cost of producing a complete wristwatch—case, frame/dial, bracelet, hands, packaging, and warranty papers—was 25 Swiss francs. To reach a production cost of less than 10 Swiss francs, that is, a reduction of more than 60%, one thing was certain: It was not enough to rely on past experiences in order to make improvements. It was necessary to start from scratch and design a completely new watch. Certain design risks would have to be taken in order to obtain such an important reduction of the production cost.

Let us take another look at the supposedly simple character of "being able to make a watch." The challenge of the conception of the product and of the process is noncore business for ETA. The activity of the company was not in the field of design-production/manufacture-distribution of finished products. We must bear in mind that in 1980, ETA was a specialized firm making watch movements and not finished watches (which it did not sell),[*] a consequence of the division of labor inherited from the cartelization of the Swiss watchmaking industry. Some companies were specialized in movement parts, others in the assembling of the movements, and others in the final assembly. The division of labor had made ETA a company specialized in the subassembly of the watch. Historically, each brand of watch made parts and integrated the majority of activities of the chain of value of watchmaking. During the 1920s, a reorganization period, the brands separated themselves from the parts. With the Swatch, ETA had to scale up, having to make a complete watch, for the first time. The Swatch "was born out of the fierce willpower of a group of engineers who were not allowed to make watches."[†] Not only was the Swatch going to be made in Granges, but ETA was going to have to distribute it and sell it, despite the fact the firm had no network and no marketing department. In other words, ETA did not possess the required knowledge when the design project was launched.

"Our main advantage lay in the fact that we were free to do what we wanted. There was no need to recycle parts of existing watches. We were free to choose the different options of design in order to reach our objectives," sums up E. Mock. The path that lay ahead for the project was steep and tortuous. But as we will see later on, it was possible to reduce by half the number of constitutive components of the watch, to simplify the final assembly, and to work on strong and controllable subunits. A constant obsession always haunted the designers: to totally automate the production of the watch.

2.3.2 Carte Blanche *for a Black Case, or Perfect Peace for Two Dissidents*

Once ETA had decided to start the Vulgaris project, it was the beginning of a long and painful journey for the two young engineers. They

---

[*] However, ETA had already made finished watches in the past with the four models of the Delirium.

[†] *L'Impartial*, 23/09/1985.

had nothing to lose and were bent on inventing a watch in the most simple and efficient way possible. The initial planning was quite optimistic, anticipating the beginning of sales in early 1982. "I was only 26 years old; in the worst-case scenario, I would have found myself another job. Jacques also decided to take the plunge," remembers E. Mock. For the two designers, the project did not represent a risk but, on the contrary, an amazing opportunity to play, to learn, and to make their dreams come true. Nevertheless, Mock and Müller would be all on their own at the start of the project, as nobody wanted to work with them. Nobody took the risk of working with these "two crazy guys who were definitely going to mess up," at a time when so many people were being sacked in the watchmaking sector. All the signs were clear: The two young engineers and all those who would join them on this project of the iconoclastic watch would be the next employees to be sacked.

Thomke relieved the two engineers of all their other duties, allowing them six months to develop the watch. Mock and Müller had to report directly to Thomke and were given high-priority access to all resources. From then on, Mock and Müller worked relentlessly. Nobody interfered in what they were doing. The very name of Thomke opened all doors and protected the two inventors from all suspicious, hostile, and defeatist attitudes. Willy Salathé, Director of Engineering at ETA, was the go-between for Thomke and the project. An internal memo dated August 29, 1980, recommended total discretion within the ASUAG group concerning the Vulgaris project and especially concerning ASULAB (the R&D department of ASUAG), which did not look kindly on the attempts of the two dissidents of Granges.[*]

A "Vulgaris dossier," dated July 1, 1980, and written by J. Müller, reviewed the situation and described eight technical options possible for the watch. This highly technical dossier systematically compared the pros and cons of each option. Six months went by and nothing happened. It was only in December 1980 that the first drawings were produced; but it was necessary to wait yet another six months to make the first prototype of the watch, whose hands turned backwards due to an engineering mistake . . . !!!!! "We made a few mistakes concerning the fine details." It was

---

[*] E. Mock remembers E. Thomke telling him and his colleague J. Müller "to be wary of ASULAB who will not look favourably at the attempts underway. Keep attentive but do not speak . . . only make small talk."

on the basis of this prototype that Thomke started the first real marketing operation (see infra). On December 23, 1981, the first five Swatches were completed and working. They were injection-molded on the famous Netstal machine and hand assembled. But after only just five days, all the watches stopped working. Nonetheless, Ernst Thomke continued to stand by the project, claiming that "if we have five watches that work for five whole days then we are almost there."

It was at that precise moment that he decided to launch the project once and for all, with the aim of distributing 10,000 Swatches on the American market from the autumn of 1982 onward. At this point in time, the development of the Swatch had already cost 800,000 Swiss francs, but the commercial and industrial investments would be much more significant. It would take another six months to perfect the marketing concept as well as the design before launching the Swatch worldwide. The project would finally be completed in three years, when the Swatch was launched on the European market on March 1st (see Figure 2-2).

What was proposed at the beginning of 1980 did not exist elsewhere. Mock and Müller were proposing something different—"something totally impossible!"—was what was soon to be heard by the watchmakers of ETA while the project progressed. ETA was the very incarnation of the world of beautiful mechanics. This was a dirt cheap watch made of plastic that desecrated the identity of the watch itself and of all traditional

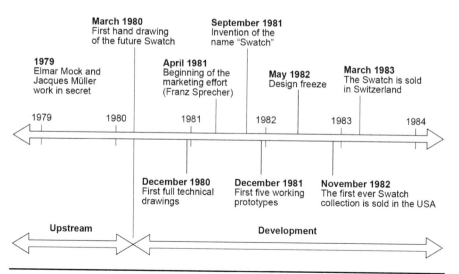

Figure 2-2   Timeline of the Swatch Project.

designers. "We have never made a million times the same watch before; nobody would want to buy that sort of product!" was what was heard in the sector. The majority of watchmakers did not want the Swatch and would only finally accept it when their ships were sinking. Teased by the "happy few"—"we were treated like gravediggers, working against the tradition of Swiss prestige"—Mock and Müller worked towards the concept of a watch that did not exist, not yet anyway. . . .

2.4 The Innovative Design of the Swatch

In an interview published by the *Harvard Business Review*, N. Hayek explained that "the Swatch is not only an engineering triumph but also a creative one" (Taylor, 1993). We will now explain how it was both at the same time. A concept cannot exist without knowledge and vice versa. Imagination or creativity alone was not enough to invent the Swatch because it was not simply a work of art but rather an industrial product that cost very little to manufacture (being mass-produced in a sector where this had never been done before). Conversely, a feat of engineering could never have produced such a trendy designer product as the original knowledge of the engineers was limited to what Hayek called "an ugly plastic watch" (Ibid.). The engineers were also key players in the conceptual phase, and creative people were involved in the engineering phase. Instead of simply listing the technical and conceptual innovations of the Swatch, we will use the theoretical framework of the design called "C-K" in order to tell the story of the conception of the Swatch as a surprisingly structured form of thinking (see Table 2-4).

Table 2-4 C-K Theory (Concept—Knowledge, a First Approach)

C-K is a theory of innovative design that studies and represents designer reasoning. Up until very recently, in the world of research there was no theory of innovative design. C-K is, therefore, a decisive breakthrough. As a unified theory, it proposes a rigorous systematic approach to creative design that can be at least used to retrace *ex post facto* the lines of reasoning behind the design. The reasoning of innovative design obeys a rigorous and unexpected rationality that the C-K Theory represents in a simple and efficient manner.

The C-K Theory was originally developed at the Ecole des mines de Paris, during the mid-1990s, at the initiative of professors Armand Hatchuel and Benoît Weil, of the Centre de Gestion Scientifique (Hatchuel and Weil, 2003). It is based on the empirical observation of practices and processes of design,

---

(*Continued from previous page*)

in order to model random, risky "things" that are emerging and helping these practices and processes to occur.

C-K is based on the distinction between two spaces of design: C space of concepts (the imaginary, proposals of the incredible and of the unknown, such as the space of "watches that do not exist") and the K space of knowledge held by the head managers of the company, by the suppliers, and even by the most distant of stakeholders. The design process is characterized by the going to and fro of the two spaces. C-K takes into account not only the origin of concepts and their transformations, by defining the design as the coevolution of the C+K spaces. Without a concept, no new knowledge is possible, and without any previous knowledge, the concepts cannot emerge. The C-K Theory wants to avoid the restrictions placed on the space of knowledge (e.g., innovation comes out of the application of scientific knowledge) or on the space of concepts (innovation is reduced to creativity). It is the joint expansion that is reciprocally determined by the two spaces that provokes the production of concepts (C) and *in fine* of unknown objects, from the knowledge experienced (see diagram below).

The C-K Theory takes into account the proliferation of new knowledge, of creative surprises, of new concepts, of the variety of alternatives. It allows "the possibility to go beyond the aporias of the design considered to be the solution to the problems, even if they are creative" (Le Masson, 2008, p. 22) and clarifies the way one can arrive at the type of reasoning that leads to innovation. It explains how it is possible to design something from the unknown, clarifying the processes that lead to creativity and to the learning process in the design.

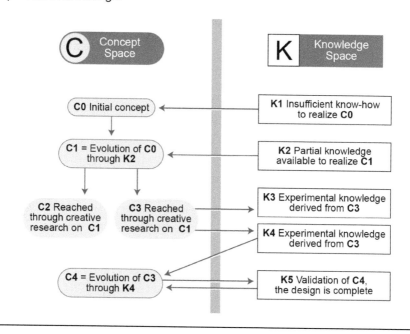

It is the very design of the watch itself and its manufacturing process that differentiated the Swatch from the other watches. Without going into any technical details, a few essential points of reference will be provided to help the reader who is unfamiliar with the watchmaking world.

The initial concept (C0) was defined as follows by E. Thomke, E. Mock, and J. Müller in April 1980:

- A Swiss quality watch (and not just watch movements)
- Inexpensive (less than 10 Swiss francs; a 60% price reduction)
- A mass-produced watch based on an automated process
- Swiss made

Regarding the knowledge space, there is indeed what we will define in the next chapter as a "disjunction," that is to say an initial gap between the formulated concept and the knowledge that allows it to happen. In short, we had no idea as to how we should go about doing it! Indeed, the knowledge of the Swiss watchmaking industry at the beginning of the 1980s was not organized around cheap watches nor around mass-produced ones. Nevertheless, the knowledge space was not totally void when the project was launched.

- On the one hand, all the "mockian" experimentations and learning had developed the K's in plastics by studying the manufacturing processes; this knowledge would very rapidly retroact on the design of the watch itself.
- On the other hand, the other K's of the "technical object watch" emerged during the original discussions between Mock and Müller. The latter, thanks to his professional background, had become an expert on inexpensive watches and, in particular, concerning their materials and their micromechanical assembly. These K's would be gradually formalized, first from a technical perspective and then in terms of marketing and design, thanks to the arrival of new people on the project.

It is now necessary to look at how the product was invented from the merging of three successive sources of knowledge. The first experimented around the plastics process, which gave rise to the product itself. The conception of its structure, its marketing, and the design of the watch itself would come later, with the involvement of new colleagues who brought with them new knowledge. Finally, the industrial process as such would be designed when it was time to move into mass-production. At each stage, knowledge interacted with concepts.

2.4.1 From the Knowledge of the Plastics Process to the Expanding of the Initial Concept

The design of the Swatch began, as already shown, with the experimentation and the studies by E. Mock of plastic materials and their processes. Here, the innovation of the product resulted from the innovation of the *process*, in contrast with the teaching of classical theories of innovation (Utterback and Abernathy, 1975). It was the acquisition of the new knowledge gained from the manufacturing process that would allow for the new watch to be defined.

The discoveries learned from the use opened up three directions simultaneously:

- The assembly of the plastic, that is, the means of keeping all the different plastic parts together; this know-how was a result of research in soldering, gluing, and brazing.*
- The plastic injection: The injection molding was a mass-production manufacturing technique of parts, which used injection-molding machines to soften the raw plastic by warming up or heating before injecting in a mold and finally cooling down for solidification.
- The coloring of the plastic, be it the mastering of the color or the printing of the patterns on the plastic (see Table 2-5).

---

* Soldering permanently assembles objects thanks to the fusion of two materials that recreate a homogeneous body during the liquid phase that solidifies when it cools down, thereby creating a continuous and homogeneous entity. Brazing is a form of welding that entails assembling by using a material different from the assembled pieces—that is, using an intermediary alloy. In contrast with soldering, fusion does not necessarily happen with brazing. Gluing is the junction wherein the fixation of the materials or the objects is obtained with glue.

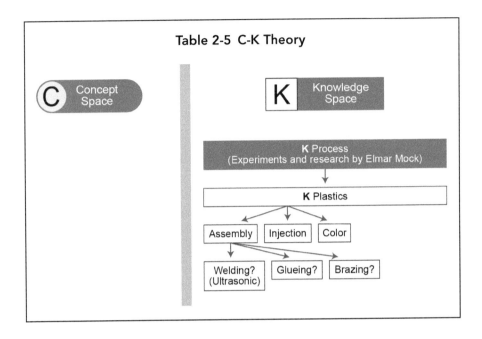

Table 2-5 C-K Theory

The plastics engineering studies that E. Mock completed in 1978 prepared him for his future experimentations with plastics as well as for the design process. During his studies, E. Mock discovered technologies that were unusual as well as foreign to the watchmaking industry, and he discovered *a contrario* their general uses in other sectors. In 1980, plastic injection and ultrasound welding[*] were not used that much in the watchmaking industry,[†] in contrast with other sectors, such as the car sector, which used it massively. Because E. Mock had learned how to weld car indicators and lights, he was able to experiment and learn solutions concerning the enclosing of glass in plastic on the case of a plastic-injected watch. Once he had completed his studies, he met up with a lot of plastics suppliers and, in particular, with Branson, the

---

[*] The ultrasound welding machine produces high-frequency vibrations (more than 20kHz) thanks to a vibrating tool called an ultrasonic horn. These vibrations are applied to two parts (in this case, polymers), and the welding is done at their interface, thanks to the transformation of the mechanical energy into heat. The ultrasound welding is a rapid and economical assembly for heat-sensitive materials such as plastic.

[†] Small insulation parts could already be made of plastic for certain watches.

manufacturer of the plastic welding machine, who would lend him the machines. E. Mock was also inspired by the design of compasses: Some were welded by ultrasound with a liquid inside. Here we have a concept—how to lock in a liquid in a watertight case—in keeping with his knowledge* of ultrasound welding.

After numerous trials and discussions, the ultrasound technology came out on top, even if it had always been at the heart of many a technical debate since the start of the project. The "Vulgaris dossier" of July 1, 1980, included a summary memo from E. Mock on the different properties of the plastic used for the Vulgaris. Another document from the same period presented the state of the knowledge of the possibilities of closing and welding the watch. ETA would progressively endow itself with new plastics knowledge and, above all, learn how to use it. The summary of July 1980 presented at length the different qualities of the plastic, both from a mechanical point of view and from the economical, functional, and industrial points of view. The suppliers as well as the advantages and the disadvantages of each solution were discussed. For example, the plastics that incorporate carbon fiber have good mechanical properties but are more expensive and possess a certain electrical conductivity that may disturb the functioning of the watch: They will eventually be put aside. The final decision about the plastics process was made at the end of 1980. And on August 12, 1982, almost a year and a half after the launching by E. Thomke of the Vulgaris project, the patent (CH 650894) of a "watch that includes a case made of plastic and plexiglass and a fixing procedure of the plexiglass on the case of the watch" was filed. The ultrasound welding springs out as a totally new technology in the watchmaking field.

The choice of ultrasound will interface with the space of concepts by clarifying the initial concept, C0, in two fields of activity†: (1) A watch that is "resilient and waterproof"; and (2) "an irreparable watch." This choice will also, in an original way, help to fulfill the requirements for the C0 about the production cost at 10 Swiss francs (see Table 2-6).

---

* We will use and define the term "conjunction" in the next chapter.
† This "detail" will be defined later on in Chapter 3 by the term "expansive-partitions."

Table 2-6 C-K Theory

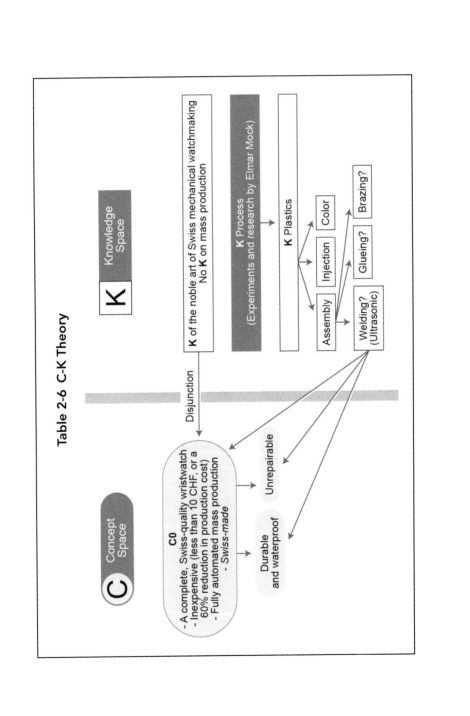

2.4.2 A Plastic-Welded Watch (Knowledge) That Is Consequently Inexpensive (Concept)

Ultrasound welding helped to mount the plexiglass on the watch (here, it is in plastic) and on the case (injection-molded plastic), and to attach various parts inside instead of using screws or other inserts. Ultrasound welding allowed for the use of less-expensive plastic—6 centimes cost price per piece of glass (injection-molded plexiglass) instead of 50 centimes (thermos-formed plexiglass)—which is 8 times cheaper. The reason was simple: Without welding, it was necessary to glue or to compress the glass by using more expensive plastics capable of withstanding pressure and the attack of solvents. The plastic of the case, weldable with injected plexiglass, chosen by E. Mock, was ABS—a material used, for example, to make Lego cubes. It was an ordinary material, highly conventional, and with no respectability from the traditional watchmaker's point of view, but it offered aesthetic qualities (brilliance, easy to color) and resilience. The case of the Swatch was made using a pressurized injection process. The high level of precision required for the case, designed to receive the preassembled parts of the watch in the mounting phase, made the development of this process one of the most difficult stages in the design of the Swatch. With any conventional watch, the cost of the casing (case, glass, hands, base) represented 50% of the total cost; with the Swatch, the proportion dropped to less than 8%. It will be shown that there were other ways of reducing cost, starting with the structure of the product itself.

2.4.3 A Plastic-Welded Watch (Knowledge) That Is Consequently Resilient and Waterproof (Concept)

Welding glass ensured an unparalleled water-resistance, while significantly reinforcing the mechanical resistance of the watch. In other words, the welded glass to the injection-molded case provides the whole with an extreme rigidity and ensures the precision of the movement inside the watch. This design was new: The glass had a mechanical function. It became a structural element of the case instead of just being a simple cover. Finally, the Swatch made up a plastic whole, resilient and waterproof, completely welded and assembled in one single block but impossible to dismantle and to repair.

2.4.4 A Plastic-Welded Watch (Knowledge) That Is Consequently Unrepairable (Concept)

Because the watch was welded it could not be repaired, and, therefore, the manufacturing process had to be flawless. A good product would not need to be repaired. All disassembling increased the complexity of the object and added a supplementary potential source of error in manufacturing. The characteristic of the Swatch being in one piece and, thus, unrepairable, meant that the mastery of the manufacturing and of the mass-production should be much higher. This was a constraint, a sentencing of the firm to strive for total quality, something the inventors took advantage of in order to improve the performance of the process and the quality of the watch. As will be shown later on, the quality of the Swatch was based on a simplified framework and on a reduced number of parts. The design circle was an exemplary one: a welded watch → irreparable → flawlessly built → running without any loss of energy or failure thanks to a simplified framework → relation of production costs of the watch → improved reliability of the process. And then, again, what would be the point of repairing a watch that only cost 5 Swiss francs which is *in fine* the production cost of the Swatch?

Moreover, the "zero fault" manufacturing got rid of the expensive links of the value chain. Admittedly, during the long and difficult development of the Swatch (cf. infra) expensive industrial corpses were spawned: Any watch that did not comply with the desired level of quality was scrapped—since it could not be repaired—whereas with dismountable watches, a part was salvageable in the event of a fault. But, as the industrial process of the Swatch became more and more reliable, all the logistics of the spare parts and the whole of the maintenance chain and the after-sales service were simply eliminated! No more stocking of spare parts; no more repair service. This was a split of identity with the traditional Swiss watch that represented durability: a watch for life. Indeed, up until then, quality Swiss watches had to be dismountable in order to cater to the after-sales service and to guarantee a certain amount of sustainability concerning the customer's purchase. On top of that, when the Tissot network was contacted in the hope that it would distribute the Swatch, it refused to sell an irreparable watch. "For us, this stand was not necessary since the most basic repair cost more than 50 Swiss francs if you took into account the logistics, the billing, and the contribution of at least one qualified person. It was better to replace the faulty product with a new one," underlines E. Mock. The engineers found an ally with Franz Sprecher, the marketing man behind the Swatch, who asked the question: "Why do you need to make a watch repairable if it works?" The tradition of repairing, however, helped the Swatch at the time of launching: The Swiss, the first consumers of the Swatch, experienced the faults of the first series. Used to taking the faulty products to the repair shop (the Swatch was guaranteed for two years), these consumers helped, unwittingly, to improve the reliability of the manufacturing process, which changed as the watches were being returned.

Finally, the concept of irreparability was a strong innovation for the Swatch, which was understandable in the relationship between the "Knowledge of Process" and the "Concept of the Product." The engineers of the Swatch intentionally created the irreparable concept of the product as a consequence of the choice of the plastics manufacturing process.

2.4.5 From the Knowledge of the Product to the Growth of the Initial Concept

If the marketing and design knowledge seemed to be more familiar to this sector than the knowledge about welding that was brought by E. Mock, they were, however, foreign to a firm that made watches, such as ETA. However, it was essential to acquire this knowledge from the outside. Once obtained this knowledge would add an aesthetic dimension to the initial C0 concept, thereby creating a fashion product at the outset of the huge commercial success of the innovation. As for the framework of the watch, its design would use original knowledge and ensure, in return, the significant reductions in manufacturing costs mentioned in the initial concept C0 (see Table 2-7).

2.4.6 A Redefined Framework: A Simpler and More Reliable Watch

The first "barroom discussion" between the two young engineers contributed a good deal to the redesigning of the interior framework of the watch: How far could they go in simplifying it? It was not a question of

Table 2-7 C-K Theory

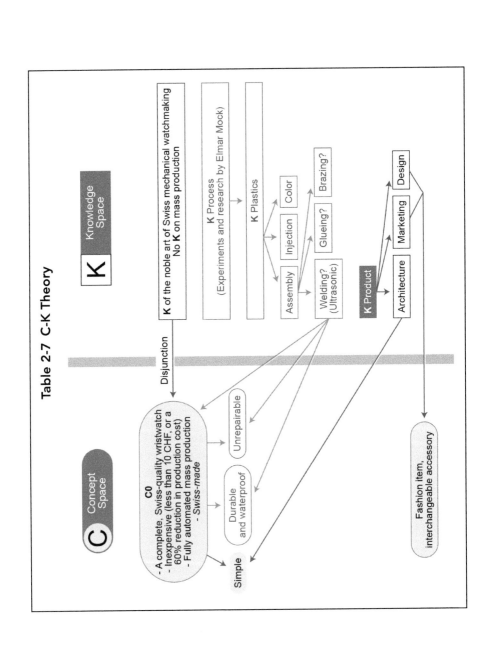

reducing, in a homothetic manner, the number of parts and connections, but more a question of the framework of the watch itself. E. Mock and J. Müller would manage to condense a maximum number of functions down to a minimum number of parts, in a steady, inexpensive, and mass-produced way. To achieve that target, they simplified, eliminated, and reused different parts. J. Müller's experience with cheap watches was precious in this phase. From the usual 150 parts for a traditional mechanical watch and 91 for a quartz watch, the Swatch was made up of only 51 parts. This result was possible because of a huge conceptual effort that was to create a double effect:

- The reduction in the number of parts made the product more reliable and simplified its production—proof that the knowledge of the process and of the product were synchronous, since they mutually defined one another.
- The reduction of the number of parts directly contributed to the reduction of the production cost (which validated the initial concept).

What was involved in the redesign of the framework of the Swatch? Quartz watches were composed of three parts: (1) a case (middle, base, and fixed glass); (2) an assembled part on a plate*; and (3) a dial and hands. In other words, once the dial had been fixed, the movement was lodged in a case that was closed afterwards with a glass (from above) and /or from a base (from below). The movements were made up of a plate on which the wheels were mounted, the gears, the mechanical parts, and various bridges and struts along with the electronic circuit. Everything was fixed mechanically to the case. Taking the mobile elements "in a sandwich," a traditional watch was thus conceived as a series of bridges and multilayered cogs, like a cruise ship. This design was too complex and too multilayered for an automatized process; the robots could not substitute the dexterity of the workers—a traditional watch was made from above, from below, and from the sides (Figure 2-3; Müller and Mock, 1983).

With the Swatch, the traditional framework was put aside in favor of a case whose bottom was also meant to support the movement; this is what was known as a "bâti-fond." In other words, the moving parts were attached to the watch case, thus eliminating the bridges. As in a car,

---

* A plate is a base part on which all other movement parts are assembled.

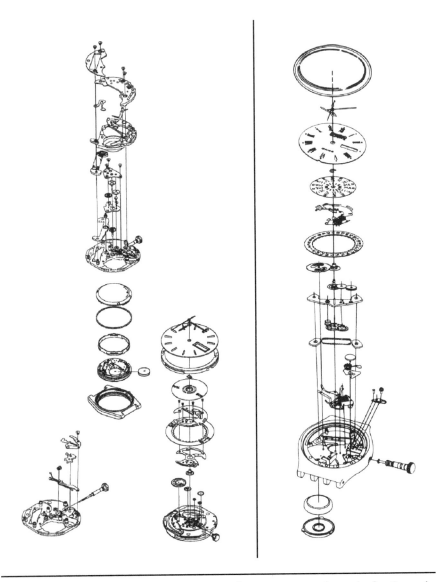

Figure 2-3 Comparison of the parts of a quartz watch and of a Swatch. Assembly technique of a watch in the early 1980s and still today (**L**) (91 components assembled from above, from below, and from the sides) versus the Swatch (**R**) (51 components fitted from above only). (*Source:* Müller and Mock, 1983)

where a chassis is replaced by a self-supporting body, the parts of the watch movement were directly attached to the case. This idea of using the base of the case as a means to assemble the components of the movement was not new, since it goes back to the 19th century. It was particularly used for the watch Delirium Tremens, which some people think, and wrongly so, is the precursor of the Swatch.* The use of the bâti-fond simplifies and enhances the reliability of the industrial assembly process, reducing the number of parts as the watch could only be mounted from above. Moreover, the bâti-fond case is made of injected plastic and incorporates all the necessary fixation systems necessary for the other parts of the watch. The use of ultrasound welding reduced the number of fixations, traditional tapping, screws, and other metallic fixation rivets inside the case. The bâti-fond received a first module, the electronic grill that was riveted by the ultrasound at the base of the case, thereby economizing the number of heavy and expensive fixation elements. On top of all of this, the coil was fixed and then the engine module, which carried the divider train of gears "which allowed us to get rid of the combination of plastic with metal, which was the cause of all kinds of important thermal expansions" (Müller and Mock, 1983). Falling back on ultrasound contributed to the reduction in the number of fixation pieces in the case, which also helped optimize the manufacturing cycle. E. Mock and J. Müller were to spend a great deal of time designing a new engine before eventually simplifying an existing one. The engine directly dragged the wheel of the second hand, and the whole was riveted by ultrasound. A supplementary wheel and the disk of the day (the date of the month) are held in place by a steel plate.

The patent (CH 643704) of March 6, 1981, sums up the work of the simplified design of the Swatch, mentioning "an electronic analogical display watch, that presents a simplified framework, which is easy to manufacture and to mass-produce, and which presents a relatively reduced thickness that still allows for a large spacing between the different components in order to increase the reliability of the watch."

---

* This detail led to many a publication that linked the Swatch to the watch Delirium Tremens. There is, of course, a sequence in time in the order of the projects—the Delirium preceded the Swatch. But apart from the bâti-fond, the Swatch was based on an original framework and had nothing to do with the Delirium. On top of that, the principle of the bâti-fond preceded the Delirium. It is more precise to say that E. Mock and J. Müller mastered the techniques of watchmaking and reused solutions that were commonplace, but they adapted them to their project.

2.4.7 The Advent of Marketing Knowledge or the Fashion Dimension

"With Jacques Müller, we wanted to make a mass-market product capable of competing with the Asian watchmakers. Jacques and myself were obsessed with the production cost and wanted to regain market shares at the low end. It was a combat watch meant for Asia, Africa, and South America," explains E. Mock. But why would anyone want to buy a cheap watch? The price argument was not a sufficient one; for the Swatch to sell it needed to be associated with a new concept. This concept was to come from outside of the ETA firm, and it was going to be imported knowledge.

Because of the division of labor in the watchmaking cartel and the specialization of ETA in watch parts, the structure of this industry, in general, and that of ETA, in particular, it was not at all prepared to confront the rationalization of the industrial machine and, even less so, in definition of a globalized strategy of marketing. That is the reason why the Swatch project outsourced its marketing. In April 1981, E. Thomke called in an independent marketing designer, Franz Sprecher, in order to add the consumer dimension to the project. The marketing plan would not question the design of the Swatch, but would use the concepts and knowledge of engineering, conferring it with a new vision. Franz Sprecher explained from the outset that the price argument was not enough to make the product exist, as the Japanese already offered cheap products. However, these cheap watches were of very poor quality and had no distinctive design. F. Sprecher, therefore, believed that the best way to sell the watch was to position it as a fashion item and not as a cheap timepiece. We change our shirt and our tie, so why not change our watch (see Figure 2-4)? The Swatch needed to be colorful in order to stand out from the crowd. The mind-blowing design and the limitless variations of the watches would appear (much) later on, after the suggestion of the number one American distributor, Bloomingdale's, which, after the flop of the first commercialization of the product in the United States, in 1982, requested a broader and trendier collection with more design that should be renewed every six months (Müller and Mock, 1983; Trueb, 2005).

Franz Sprecher and Ernst Thomke would transform the watch into an interchangeable accessory similar to a tie or a pair of earrings. The Swatch was "[f]ashion that ticks," according to Sprecher. This was a fundamental

Figure 2-4 Drawing of Swatch—fashion accessory. (*Source:* Müller and Mock, 1983)

turning point that would make the technical object an innovation, a fashion item. Sprecher enriched the original concept of the Swatch, shifting it around, developing it, and, at the same time, positioning himself as a true visionary strategist behind a watch and accessory that was to become well-known worldwide. Two specialists of the Swatch presented an approach to the concept that was inspired by the first interactions between Thomke and Sprecher, in the form of an oxymoron (the phrase is ours): "[A] watch is not a watch, a 'non-watch,' which is, at the same time, classical and futurist, from the past and from the future, a crazy watch that is anchored in technical reality (. . .) which can satisfy all publics, from the most modest to the most prestigious" (Komar and Planche, 1995, p. 15). This was no substitute product—that is, a mere copy of a Rolex. It was an innovation in its own right. The Swatch was a watch that was not a watch, that is why oxymorons were needed in order to define innovative concepts—they opened up the space of conception in opposition to to the approach of improving the existing one (a flatter watch, more beautiful, in stone, square . . .). Moreover, the oxymoron allowed us to combine different or unknown features (we've never seen anything like it!) with the known properties (but it's a watch with a bracelet, hands, and a dial). The Swatch was different; it was a redesign of the watch. Furthermore, an essential prerequisite of the concept was to seriously question what a watch does, which was previously considered as taken for granted, but preserving at the same time its classic properties in such a manner that they were still visible to the customer! The oxymoron hit home! (See Table 2-8.)

F. Sprecher also considered the product as a part of an unending experience, with a perpetually renewable life cycle thanks to the recurrent launching on the market of the new Swatches. This approach was new, at a time when the life cycle of a product was clearly limited to a certain period of time, but without any redefining of the product itself. "The commercial success of the Swatch was possible thanks to the marketing genius of Franz Sprecher and of Max Imgrüth, nicknamed 'Mad Max.' It was they who understood that the Swatch was not meant as a replacement of the Roskopf watches in third world countries but it was destined to become a lifestyle item. . . ." (Trueb, 2010). The Swatch was going to embrace all things fashionable. As N. Hayek cleverly summed up, "The Japanese inundate the low-price watch market. However, they do not possess our culture and capacity to innovate. Our team created the ugly plastic watch and we gave it all our creative talent: bright colours, provocation, clean images, without any frills attached" (Taylor, 1993).

Table 2-8 The Name "Swatch"

It was in New York, in September 1981, that the watch was baptized Swatch, an original name—a contraction of the word Swiss and watch—easy to remember and to pronounce in all languages. It is not a second watch, as suggested in certain texts, as this merely reduces the watch to the status of a replacement product of the first watch. It is an innovation in its own right, carried by a name that distinguishes it completely, and is an idea of Franz Sprecher. During the summer of 1981, he worked with an American advertising agency (Lintass SSC&B) that was used to abbreviating in their documents the Swiss watch to Swatch. And that's how the Vulgaris became the Swatch. It was as simple as that! E. Thomke wanted to protect the name straightaway, but ran into a problem: All watches made in Switzerland can pride themselves on being a Swiss watch. However, he was lucky, because in the United States, the word swatch meant cloth coupons in the fashion world. The name could be protected, and the product was baptized.

The distribution of the watch was also a part of the design process. It is to be remembered that Swiss retailers did not want to sell the plastic watch straightaway. "We tried everything," explained E. Thomke, "from major brands of related products with their own distribution networks to the supermarkets, not forgetting the sports retailers or hard discount stores, everybody refused to work with us. Nevertheless, with the consequent success of the Swatch, they would all finally end up begging for it. . . ."*

2.4.8 From the Knowledge of Design to an Expanded Concept and a Discreetly Efficient Product

Once the framework of the watch had been decided upon by E. Mock and J. Müller, there was the question of the design (in the strict sense of the shape). The fashion twist suggested by F. Sprecher influenced the choice of the external shape of the Swatch, which shows how much work was involved between the "Design Knowledge" and the "Design Concept."

The designers were told not to copy the metallic dials that were the reference at that period of time. The metal ersatz was popular back then and was precisely the pitfall to be avoided. How do you go about making plastic a valued material? In order to do so, the designers needed to propose neutral shapes for the case, that is to say, like water—colorless, odorless, and insipid—the design of the Swatch would stick out because of its lack of character. The watch had to be discreet in its simplicity and the neutrality of its design in order to avoid annoying anyone. The case, with its lack of charisma and boldness, should not draw attention to itself; its docile shape should be easily accepted. This was the strength of the design! The perfect neutrality of the shape would allow the watch to be paired to all graphic styles.

E. Thomke used knowledge available outside ETA as well as within the organization. For the record, the two initial designers who were to work simultaneously on the project were G. Coulin and Hans Zaugg. The first was a designer from Metal Product AG, one of the firms that had recently been taken over by ETA as a part of E. Thomke's general reorganization plan. G. Coulin produced a hundred sketches and defined

---

* Taken from an interview of E. Thomke by Gilles Garel during the preparation of this book.

a lyre shape that still possessed a great deal of character. Hans Zaugg was an external designer. He had no background in watches but was from the interior design and furniture world.* He belonged to the tradition of minimalist design and thus produced timeless sketches with a pure and neutral shape for the dial of the watch. A prototype of the watch was created with this design. Finally, at the end of the six months deadline that had been defined by E. Thomke at the very start of the project, all the technical and aesthetic principles of the Swatch were defined. The management of ETA approved and established the well-known lyre shape of the Swatch. A huge amount of work remained to be done on the design of the case, the glass, the hands, the bracelet, and the dial.

The creators of the final artistic design of the Swatch were Maryse Schmid and Bernard Müller (the brother of Jacques)—both freelancers. Their story is told at great length in the book *Swatchissimo* (Carrera, 1991). At the start of the project, E. Thomke rejected the dials, as they were too original and fanciful, and could potentially turn the future watch into a simple plastic gadget. Müller and Schmid finally produced an excellent design for the Swatch, at the same time simple and upscale. The male and female models took on the shape of "something so pure and functional that the aesthetic side clearly emerged like a sort of eternal value. The efficiency and the discretion of the design of the parts reinforced the solidity of the product, the waterproofness and the clarity of the dial thereby becoming the most important element, at the heart of all the never ending creative expressions of a certain period" (Komar and Planche, 1995, p. 13). It was no longer a movement that was encased but rather an encasing with hands that moved. Special attention was paid by Schmid and

---

* Let's take a look at more recent times, and in another sector, at the case of Apple, which found its pearl of a design thanks to Jonathan Ive. Ive started off at Tangerine, a small design consultancy in London that he founded in 1990. Two years later, Apple employed the creative people of his company in order to imagine the lines of the future range of laptops. Ive was working on a line of bathrooms for Ideal Standard when he came up with the design for the Powerbook. His design for the furniture was rejected, but his work for the Powerbook was most impressive. Apple employed Ive, who moved to California. He became the head of the Industrial Design Department of Apple a few months before the return of Steve Jobs. After the launch of the iMac, all Apple products were redesigned.

Müller to the perfecting of the balance between the shapes and the joints and the exterior parts. They created a minimalist design product.

The plastics know-how, combined with the creativity of the designers, worked well in relation to the colors of the watch. Basically the engineers had to share with the designers their knowledge of plastics and its characteristics, along with the manufacturing process. Conversely, the constraints of the designers needed to be assimilated by the experts in plastic injection-molding, even if, at the time, nobody imagined the profusion of colors, styles, and variety of design series of the Swatch that would follow. E. Mock coached the designers about the physical properties of plastic, the constraints of the injection-molding technology, and the industrial colorization of plastic watches. "Bernard (Müller) learned the rudiments of plastics . . . and all about the range of materials; with his great sense of humor and a lot of intelligence, the engineer (E. Mock) dissected the plastic bodies, commented on the parts, the compatibility and incompatibility of the materials . . . Maryse (Schmid) acquired a solid background in the field in order to enlarge her research and her trials" (Carrera, 1991, p. 49). The Swatch must demold without any overhang. The tactile qualities of the plastic (the watch has a nice feel to it—soft, matte, and smooth) are a result of the sandblasting of the mold that receives the polymer resin. Here, the knowledge of the design validates the knowledge of the *process*. Conversely, after a series of unsuccessful trials of the first bracelets, it is the engineering that proposes the hinge system that made the Swatch be instantly recognized at a glance. Mock also spent a huge amount of time on making the plastic transparent (see Figure 2-5 and Table 2-9).

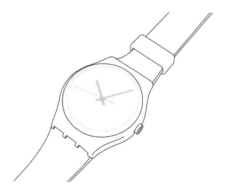

Figure 2-5   Drawing of the Swatch with a hinge bracelet.

Table 2-9 The Hinge Bracelet of the Swatch

The traditional watch bracelets are made up of a rod (or brooch) that goes through the bracelet and is fixed at the two extremities of the case of the watch. In the case of the plastic Swatch, this system created tears in the case because of the tension created by the bracelet. During Christmas 1981, 300 Zaugg watches with a traditional fixation system were tested. There was no plan to sell them; they were only meant to be worn on the wrist. But a third of them would tear, which is a high proportion. The Swatch adventure could have stopped there and then because the conditions of the watch were unsellable. On top of that, the aesthetic integration of the case with the bracelet was not perfect; depending on the width of your wrist or whether you were a man or a woman, the watch was not the same . . . But E. Thomke wanted a watch that was "beautiful for all wrists." It was necessary to innovate. In the spring of 1982, when the project was already well under way, the engineers (yet again them!) proposed a hinge system, such as the one you find on doors, which comprises the moorings. And so it is not the bracelet that is modified but the method of attaching it to the case. By introducing a four-point hinge, the pressure was reduced by a factor of 25, and the whole "case and bracelet" obtained an excellent mechanical resistance, regardless of the diameter of the wrist. The gain in resistance allowed the patenting of the hinge bracelet. The designers, B. Müller and M. Schmid, achieved an aesthetic harmony between the bracelet and the case. *In fine*, the hinge integrates itself perfectly to the overall design of the watch. The technical solution of the hinge not only had aesthetic implications, because it became a major marketing argument, consecrating the distinctive image of the watch and of the group Swatch. Later on, this visual signature was reused in all the other models of the brand (even when there was no mechanical use as, for example, in the case of steel watches) and became a typical feature of the product, while the copies of the Swatch started to reproduce the image and not the technology. Finally, the apparently simple patent of the hinge bracelet played an important part in the war against counterfeits. In C-K terms, the knowledge of the engineers created an integrated design "watch/bracelet" and of the concept of a signature or of a recognition of the product(s).

The designer Jean Robert[*] appeared on the scene after the two collections of 1984, adding a new artistic touch to the Swatch design. With Kathy Dürer, they were the first of a long list of professionals who would produce and reproduce themes for the Swatch, along with the famous Swatch Lab of Milano. In 1984, Max Imgrüth, the Marketing Director at

---

[*] J. Robert is a designer of women's stockings at the Fogal Company. He is a trained engraver as well as an expert in the art of reducing shapes. His experience brought an original, graphic eye to the Swatch.

Swatch USA, suggested that specific names for watches and collections be given. The Swatch conquered the world and the collective imagination, not as a simple, inexpensive plastic watch but as a fashion accessory that epitomized youth, prestige, sportsmanship, and the avant-garde.

2.4.9 The Design of the Process of Manufacturing

In order to understand the design of the manufacturing process of the Swatch, let's have a look at the history of the Swiss watch industry, because the leap made by the Swatch was radical. Never before had the manufacturing of a watch been totally automated, despite some historic attempts (see Table 2-10).

2.4.10 The Swatch Standardized the Production and Diversified the Product

Millions of examples of the same watch would be produced, but how do you go about selling identical watches in an industry known for its diversity? Or rather, how do you convince the market that you are producing something different (a watch for each of us and a watch for everyone), when you are making a standardized product? The specialists of the production management or the management of operations spoke of "delayed differentiation" to describe the process of manufacturing that was standardized before, but as late as possible in the production flow, certain elements of differentiation made the product unique and created value in the eyes of the customer. The same Swatch was made over and over, but the final assembly stage catered to the addition, on the same assembly line, of an abundance of printed designs, colors, and logos. The changing of only one of the four features made the Swatch unique: color, dial, hands, and date display. The creative unpredictability of the design had managed to reinvent the Swatch that continues, from a process perspective, to be a standard product and one that is very inexpensive to make.

This was a true industrial strategy choice that was made from the start—one that would profit from the engineering power of ETA, surpassing the initial efforts of E. Mock and J. Müller. The work put in to develop the process of the Swatch was indeed more important than the development of the product itself.

Table 2-10 A Historically Slightly Industrialized Industry

The Swiss watch Industry has not always been hostile to the mechanization of manufacturing. Indeed, it had to commit itself to this trend towards the end of the 19th century when faced with the competition of American companies that managed to standardize the production of watches in the new factories, by transferring the gunmaking technologies along with those needed for the making of sewing machines (Donzé, 2009, p. 26). The famous report of Jacques David and Theodor Gribi of 1876, two Swiss citizens fascinated by the American watchmaker model, promotes the mechanization and interchangeability of parts that make it possible for a huge number of watches to be made. Later on, during the period from 1920 to 1960, when the wristwatch became fashionable, Swiss production became more democratic and huge quantities of inexpensive, mechanical watches were sold.

Despite this evolution towards the mass market, marketing of the brands resolutely remains oriented around luxury and precision. The automatization was never really massive, for two main reasons. To start, manual or semi-automated manufacturing means that family jobs in the Jura area were maintained. Secondly, Swiss watch brands have always had a large width and depth to their range of products. With such a huge amount of products, templates, and materials, it is practically impossible to standardize and to automate production. On the contrary, the noble art of this industry lies in the manual know-how of the diversity of the complex products. For example, if the industrial factory at Fontainemelon produces the *ébauches* in an industrial manner, since the beginning of the 19th century it proposes roughly a thousand different mechanical models for its customers, which prevents it from truly rationalizing its production (Donzé, 2009, p. 31). "In the town of La Chaux-de-Fonds alone, there are 67 different specializations in 1870 (. . .) There are 1308 autonomous workshops in this area (. . .) small companies specialized in a very limited manufacturing process of the watch" (Ibid., p. 17).

At the end of the day, what characterizes the professional identity of this profession is the constant quest to improve the quality and the diversity of the product, rather than the rationalisation of the production process. The industrialization at the end of the 19th century is only partial; no big factories are founded, only small manufacturers or workshops. «In 1923, there were 972 factories active in the watchmaking industry who employed on average 35 people» (Ibid., p. 111). The development of the Swiss watch industry was made possible by respecting the principle of extreme specialization, with many small family companies, not very capitalized, and organized around the workbench system of «*système d'établissage*," like the industrial districts. The Swatch breaks away from this tradition by being able to integrate the standardization of the production of a complete watch.

2.4.11 From the Initial Industrial Improvisation to Mass Production

The first prototypes of December 1980 were totally assembled by hand. Eighty percent of the preassembly was automated in 1983, but the process was far from complete. The success of the Swatch, when it was launched in Switzerland, was 10 times more than was forecasted, and the industrial manufacturing machine was not ready. The first million Swatches were made by hand by 300 women working together in an assembly hall in Granges—which would, incidentally, lead to demands on the part of the social unions. Both manual and automated production processes functioned side by side for three years: Machines preassembled the small parts of the watch, and the final assembly was done by hand. Indeed, the first watches that were sold could not be automated because of all the little details that had to be solved along the production chain. It was also necessary to modify and perfect the process as the customers brought back the watches (see irreparability). It was, therefore, a co-concept product *process* that continued, even though the Swatch was already on the market! The definitive production chain only started to really work around 1985–1986.

2.4.12 An Original Product with an Original Process and Vice Versa

The entire process was automated. Half of the 51 parts (25 subsets) of the Swatch were preassembled before reaching the assembly line, composed of 12 tables, with 5 separate operations per table. There were just as many inspections as assembly operations: inspection of individual elements, of preassembled components or modules, of the assembly process before a final inspection. The Department of Quality Control of ETA even set up new data systems for calculating the required measurements. At that point, it was a truly lean production system of total quality that was achieved at a time when such policies were neither customary nor commonplace in European industry. A Swatch was produced every three seconds within a production cycle of roughly an hour. Once made, each watch was seriously tested through an automated process, and in the space of 24 hours—for waterproofness, temperature, and resistance (the

Table 2-11 C-K Theory

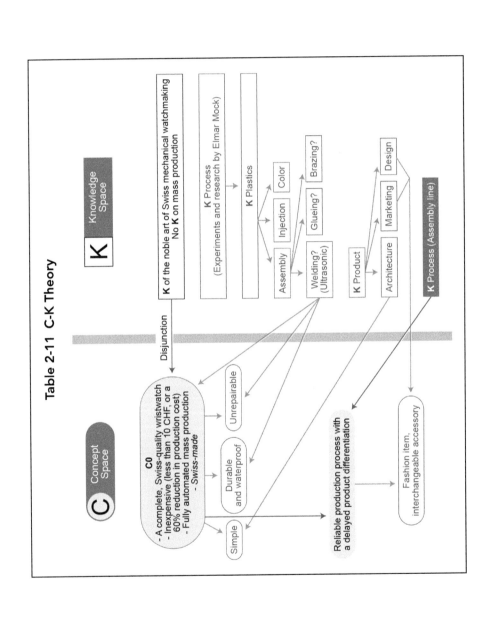

Swatch was tested at 5000G, a level at which all the low-end timepieces would fall apart when you thumped your wrist on a table). Before the final control, the components and the preassembling were checked. The complexity of this process meant that the manufacturing could remain in Switzerland, rather than being outsourced to a country with cheap labor (see Table 2-11).

From April 1980, hence at the very beginning of the project, E. Mock was in the Engineering Department of ETA, under the management of Willy Salathé, so that he could have direct access to all of the company's design resources. The department, located in Granges, merged with the one in Fontainemelon in order to create an initial strike force of a dozen engineers and technicians. At the height of the project, 200 people were involved in the development of the process. After having been the head of the Department of Materials of Engineering from 1982 to 1985, E. Mock would remain the man with the memory of the product concerning the engineering side of the manufacturing up until he left the company in 1986.

2.5 Conclusion

The final C-K arborescence of the Swatch, described here, retraces the main thinking behind the concept that ended up as an innovation. In Table 2-12, the grey rectangles in the Knowledge space distinguish three sorts of knowledge necessary for the completion of the tasks of the project.

2.5.1 The Fundamental Management Lessons to be Learned from Breakthrough Innovation

The Essential Interactions between Product and Process

In this project, it is the *process* that creates the product that creates the *process*. And yet, classic theories of innovation sequentially divide up the time of the product and the time of the *process*; first, the innovation product and then the innovation *process*. But such a disassociation is not logical:

- The simplicity of the watch, its reliability, and its low cost are a result of the constraints of the manufacturing; it is also clear that as the

Table 2-12 The C-K of the Swatch

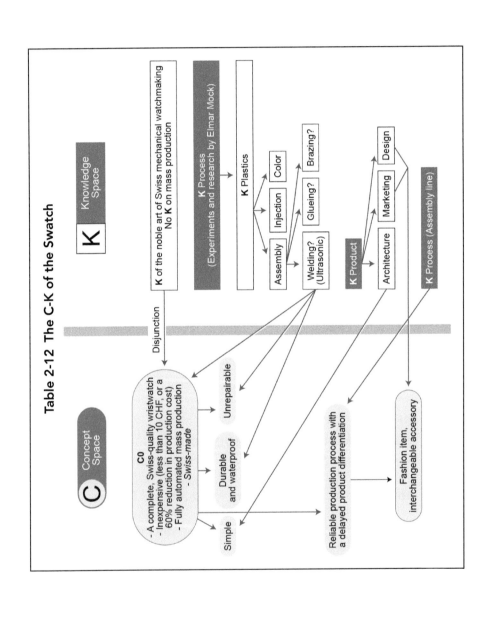

industrial *process* of the Swatch became more and more reliable, it was the concept of irreparability of the product that clearly emerged.
– On the other hand, certain properties of the product influenced the *process* choice. For example, the reduction of the number of parts simplified the manufacturing. The tactile qualities sought for in this watch (matte and soft, nice to touch plastic) forced the engineers and designers to revise the complete *process*. In this case, the knowledge of the design of the product was crucial for the choice of the processes.

With such instances of interaction between the product and the *process*, the engineers were also on the side of the concept and the creative people could also be found on the side of the know-how of engineering. In terms of design strategy for a company, this meant that a linear approach such as a *stage gate* was out of the question. In this type of strategy, milestones were defined that aimed to progressively reach the target that was decided upon from the start. On the contrary, for the production of the Swatch, the process had to be repeated and to redefine itself with this newly acquired knowledge. In terms of industrial strategy for a company, or even concerning industrial policy for a government,[*] it is obvious how important it is to know how to center the investments in the manufacturing processes while keeping an overall innovative vision of the product. The C-K tree shows how money invested directly into the process is directly linked to the properties of the product and vice versa.

2.5.2 Take the Time to Acquire the Knowledge

The start of Elmar Mock's career shows how desperately he needed to avoid all form of control, and yet he was aware that he had to play the company game by continuing to invent. At that time, F. Scholl, the Manager of ETA allowed him to work undercover, to experiment, and to play with an injection machine. The plastics knowledge vital for the Swatch would slowly come to a head between the arrival of E. Mock at ETA in 1976, followed by his plastics engineering studies in 1978, and the launching of the Vulgaris project in March 1980. Can this long period of time spent acquiring and decanting the necessary knowledge, along with

---

[*] The only federal government intervention in an industrial sector took place in the Swiss watchmaking industry in the 1930s.

the freedom enjoyed by the young employees on the payroll, still be of any relevance to companies today?

2.5.3 The Protection of a Mentor Leader

In the Swatch project, the role of the Director, E. Thomke, was not limited to just a bit of support, to a few hierarchical authorizations, and to the signing of a few investment applications. He was also the mentor, the godfather, and the guardian of the project in which he trusted, along with the inventors who had complete freedom to work. Often, specialist literature explains how innovation must be totally backed by a hierarchy that is clearly committed and involved—almost anti-managerial—a hierarchy that imposes new rules and rejects traditional management regulations. The involvement of the mentor of the innovation always involves a certain amount of risk, as he puts himself in a dangerous position, accepting the consequences of failure and yet continuing to defend the principles of iconoclastic management. Thomke put the two young gladiators in the arena, but he would never lower his thumb to finish them off, especially when the project was about to encounter difficulties.

2.5.4 Draw, Prototype, Represent

For E. Thomke, the drawing of Mock and Müller, in March 1980, arrived at the right moment while he was thinking, along with his colleagues at ETA, about "another watch." He had already questioned R&D on the subject, but they did not foresee anything tangible on the horizon. The drawing of Mock and Müller was something real, something possible! This shows how important it is for the makers of innovation to have a representation of the object to be designed that will speak to the decision makers (receptive . . .): a drawing, a model, a prototype (see Conclusion).

2.5.5 The Reuse of Familiar or Unfamiliar Knowledge

For a very long time, reuse has been a part of the many strategies of innovation. However, the reworking of something that already exists, normally hidden from the customer before a new aspect is revealed, is much more difficult. This implies a huge amount of work on the "basis of knowledge," so if you decide to do it at least "do something new."

In the case of the Swatch, much watchmaking knowledge was reused for its conception: the bâti-fond was patented in roughly 1880; inexpensive plastic watches had already been launched by Fortis, Oris, and other brands; the rod for the time set was inspired by the Cyma pendulette of the 1930s; and a simplified Lavet engine had been developed for Ebauches Bettlach. This presupposed the collecting of a huge reservoir of knowledge: "We had to know everything that existed, which implied an overall curiosity that bordered on something quite pathological," writes L. Trueb (2010) about E. Mock and J. Müller. The two engineers were not only perfectly acquainted with the latest modern technologies, they were also genealogists, historians of watchmaking techniques. As Franz Sprecher summed it up, "[Y]ou cannot discover anything great if you do not get to the bottom of things."

Some of the reused knowledge came from other fields, totally outside of the watchmaking sector. We have seen, for example, how the soldering of the plexiglass to the ABS plastic case was commonly used in car lights. The ultrasound technique would be used a lot by the Swatch in order to replace the screws, glue, rivets, and other costly inserts that characterized mechanical watches. Sometimes it is necessary to gather a lot of knowledge before you imagine the design.

Two points must be emphasized about the scope of the knowledge. On the one hand, it boils down to establishing a state of the art or rather a *state of the non-art*. The latter helped answer the question, "What don't we know?" (See Chapter 3 on the design KCP workshops.) And it revealed the weaknesses, the limits in the knowledge retained by the company. On the other hand, the task of reimporting the knowledge was a long and difficult learning process, so much so since it took place in a world unaccustomed to receiving and using this new kind of knowledge. Specialists are not always willing to question their knowledge—the same knowledge that allows them to create their professional comfort zone.

2.5.6 Putting Up with Deviant Tendencies; Preparing for the Breakthrough

When the development of the Swatch began, ETA was a company submerged by the general crisis, undermined by massive redundancy measures. In this period of chaos, the fear of tomorrow coexisted with an amazing sense of freedom. It was like being in a country where war has knocked down all the prison doors, some prisoners stay inside their cells—this is perfectly normal—whereas others decide to run off to start a new life. Somewhere along the line between the intelligent and the crazy people, between those who belong in the gas world and those in the crystal world (see Chapter 4), E. Mock and J. Müller chose which world they wanted to be in. Normally, the firm ETA was not structured to put up with deviant tendencies, but with the crisis, ETA conceded to accepting anarchistic and entrepreneurial behaviour that was on the edge. This dissident attitude must not be merely considered as a digression from what is normal, as the post-crisis period would put things back into place, but it must be seen as a sign that heralds the organization of tomorrow's concept. Indeed, E. Mock was already unconsciously preparing the creation of his future company devoted to breakthrough innovation, Creaholic.

2.5.7 Do Not Make Hasty Negative Judgments or Straightaway Think That Something Is Impossible

The development project of the Swatch was shrouded in a lot of scepticism and sarcasm because its separation from the traditional world of Swiss watchmaking was too abrupt. Plastic, huge quantities, cheap prices . . . there was no way that this could work! It was clear that the terms of the initial concept had their roots in a known universe (a watch), and, at the same time, they opened up the design space (a watch like no other). In order to innovate, the initial concept had to be accepted as it was. It must neither be judged *a priori* nor questioned immediately, but it was important to confront it with the knowledge space in order to assess it and make it evolve.

E. Thomke trusted Mock and Müller and "paid to see." When the two young engineers showed him the future Swatch in March 1980, the watch was just a vulgar drawing that could not predict what was going to happen. It was totally impossible to imagine that a caterpillar, a hairy worm, would one day be able to fly and become a beautiful butterfly. So how do you make a decision when you have no idea of what is going to happen? A lot of innovations remain cocoons, never getting past the caterpillar stage as more and more managers need to analyze the risks, wanting proof of a return on investment and the guarantee that a market does exist, and that is how they end up killing the initial concept.

2.5.8 The Commercial Launching of the Swatch

After the launching (partially forgotten) of 10,000 watches in Houston, TX, USA, in November 1982, the first Swatch—in reality a collection of twelve different models—was presented on March 1, 1983, in Zürich during a press conference at the Atlantis Hotel. E. Mock and J. Müller are present in the room.

The American launch was a commercial fiasco but a decisive learning experience that helped to differentiate this watch from all the others. The American market was in fact a test for ETA concerning the iterative process of the designing of the Swatch: work fast and efficiently, act quickly, learn and try again. Marvin Traub, CEO of the distributor, Bloomingdale's, did not want to continue promoting and selling such a product. He asked for at least twenty different models, a new collection every six months, and not only colorful watches, but also designer ones. Bloomingdale's was, therefore, the first distributor of the Swatch that would, by guiding it towards a multitude of variations, contribute to its success.

A little later the same year, the watch would be launched in the United States, Germany, and Great Britain. Whereas the American market remained indifferent to the little plastic watch, Switzerland and Europe adopted it. The initial price was somewhere between 39.90 and 49.90 Swiss francs.* The market studies estimated that it would be possible to sell, at most, 50,000 watches a year in Switzerland. In the first year, 500,000 were sold. . . .

Its price, very modest for a Swiss-made watch, along with a successful advertising campaign and above all support from the Swiss market, immediately launched the watch. "Suddenly it was not only possible to think and do things differently but we were allowed to look at it from a different point of view" (Hainard, in Carrera, p. 10). Switzerland then became aware that national watchmaking was undergoing a radical change. Six months after its launching, Konstantin Theile, in charge of

---

* The price is standardized at 50 Swiss francs in the autumn of 1993.

the marketing of the Swatch in Granges, estimated that 100,000 of the "patriotic Swatches" were sold in the Confederation. In 1984, the Swatch belonged to the twelve products acclaimed by the magazine *Fortune*. That same year, the directors of ETA fixed the annual sales objective at 100,000 units, whereas 220,000 watches had already been delivered on August 2nd.[*] In 1985, Swiss watchmaking could breathe again, according to the director of the Swiss watchmaking industry.[†] In terms of volume the sales of the Swatch exploded: 4 million watches in 1984, 8 million in 1985, 12 million in 1986, and 13 million in 1987. In 1988, 53 million watches were sold, 154 million in 1993. . . .

When the Swatch appeared on the scene, the Swiss press was very fond of the inventors Elmar Mock and Jacques Müller, who were invited everywhere to give interviews and lectures. "It's all over for the Japanese!" sneered the two companions in an interview where they are seen beaming in the photo.[‡] Let's not forget that a few months earlier, the Swiss were going through a major economic crisis and that all hope had been lost: The Swatch was doing them all so much good.

2.5.9 Time to Leave and to Move on to Something New

After the lightning launch of the watch, the two designers of the Swatch went their separate ways, and a new story of the Swatch was going to be spun: that of a commercial success along with a tale of the innovation factory, an official mythology. Jacques Müller climbed up the management ladder in the technical department of ETA, until 1985 when, following a plane crash, he spent eight months in hospital and in convalescence for many years. At that precise moment in time (2013), Jacques Müller was still working for the Swatch Group as director of one of the research laboratories—the CDNP (*Centre de développements de nouveaux produits*).

As for Elmar Mock, after the success of the Swatch continued in the field, and he developed another successful product, the Rockwatch, for Tissot (a small watch made of stone), he lost his younger brother, Stéphan,

---

[*] *Le Matin Tribune*, 23/09/1983; *Le Démocrate*, 3/10/1983.
[†] *L'Express*, 9/10/1985.
[‡] *L'Illustré*, no. 15, 1983, p. 107.

also an engineer at ETA, in the same plane crash that almost killed Jacques Müller. Elmar was an authorized representative at just under 30, with a team to lead and a good deal of responsibility. At that time, he had the impression that it would be a long while before he would relive that crazy period of creation. He felt the weight of an organization ruled by a routine that no longer satisfied his creative entrepreneurial aspirations and found himself in opposition with the new management at the head of ETA. E. Mock was no longer happy in a structure that was positioned more towards exploitation than exploration, with the objective of producing millions of perfect quality watches. He resigned from ETA in 1986 to set up his own company in Bienne—Createc—which would later become Creaholic. The Swatch did not make E. Mock rich, as he only received a bonus of 700 Swiss francs in 1983, being told at the time that this was a most generous gesture in a time of crisis. From 1986 onward, the name Elmar Mock was erased from all official communiqués concerning the success story of the Swatch.

Ernst Thomke remained in the group SMH as General Director up until 1991. In conflict with the CEO N. Hayek, Thomke did not mince his words in the Swiss press concerning the short-term culture of optimization of profits and the managing style of the new director, Hayek. "Today's SMH would never allow the Swatch to happen," he said in 1992.[*] After his departure, Hayek, without any rivals, could pass himself off as the savior of the Swiss watchmaking industry, even though Thomke, as he was leaving, reminded him that he was neither the "Messiah" nor the father of the Swatch.[†]

2.5.10 The Paternity of the Swatch

The paternity of an innovation is a complex issue, and it is always possible to go back a little bit further to its origins: without quartz, no Swatch; without Father Mock (also a watchmaker), no Elmar Mock, no Swatch, etc. As this book examines the origins of the Swatch from the emergence of its concept to the market launch, we will show how certain key players made everything possible, those who belong to the "extremely important

---

[*] *Le Pays*, 04/01/1992.
[†] Ibid.

genetic core" [according to Komar and Planche (1995, p. 20), specialists of the Swatch collections]. Elmar Mock and Jacques Müller's signatures are on the patents of the Swatch,* and the Gaia Award in 2010 put an end to the doubts concerning "fatherhood" by confirming that these two engineers are the inventors.

2.5.11 The Father and the Mothers

E. Mock and J. Müller, the technical designers, and E. Thomke, the strategist who supported them blindly, are the *primo* contributors to the Swatch. "Thomke is the father and we are the mothers," sums up E. Mock when he talks about himself and J. Müller. Without them, the Swatch would still have to be invented.

The Swiss press, local and regional, were so emotional about the Swatch saga and proud of this renewal from the end of 1982 to the beginning of 1985 that a lot of articles were written about the two inventors of the Swatch, Elmar Mock and Jacques Müller. The press reviews were praiseworthy of the watch and of its two inventors. The name E. Thomke was also very present at that time, and it comes as no surprise that the name Nicolas Hayek is missing from this true story of the invention.

As from 1985, the date when N. Hayek took over at the SMH, the press articles were less clear about the paternity of the Swatch.† A theory about the adulteration of the paternity starts to spread slowly but surely. "At the beginning, a couple fathers claimed responsibility for the baby Swatch, presented to the press in March 1983, the engineers Jacques Müller and Elmar Mock. Afterwards, it was more difficult to identify who did what among the players, designers and constructors. Some even claimed that without them the Swatch would not be what it is today. All of this proves

---

* In fact, E. Mock's name is on all seven patents that protect the Swatch, as is the name of J. Müller, apart from the one concerning the bracelet, where Alphonse Bron is associated with E. Mock.
† The first articles about the success of the Swatch and its inventors go back to a period when newspapers were not yet digitalized. The Swiss press of the time is not really consulted by the contemporary exegetes (professors, journalists, commentators, bloggers . . .) of the Swatch.

to what extent each and every one of them experienced the adventure in a very personal way."* Mock, Müller, Thomke, and Sprecher were progressively pushed into the background, in order to favor a more overall and collective analysis, making it difficult to understand where the various inputs came from. Here we have the official standpoint of the group: The Swatch is a corporate success. It is clear that the incredible takeoff of the product involved more and more people, and the subsequent success of the Swatch encouraged them to claim responsibility for it, coming forward to pose in the family photo sharing some of the limelight. The same people would have remained in the dark if the Swatch had been a flop. "Success has many fathers, failure is an orphan," N. Hayek used to say all the time.

2.5.12 The Putative Godfather

A news dispatch from Reuters on June 29, 2010, announced the death of "Nicolas Hayek, creator of the watch Swatch," who passed away the day before. There was a great deal of emotion, especially in Switzerland, where "the father of the Swatch" was an emblematic industrial leader of the Swiss watchmaking industry. The Internet site of the Swatch Group wrote that "under the leadership of Nicolas G. Hayek the Swatch Group achieved world fame (of which) one fundamental stage was without a doubt the launching of (. . .) a cheap good quality Swiss made watch that was both aesthetically and emotionally pleasing: the Swatch." There is no doubt about the birth of the little revolutionary watch that had saved the Swiss watchmaking industry at the beginning of the 1980s. Moreover, the case studies that educate the students of the best business schools are no exception, either concerning the Swatch or the "titan" who was at its origin (Taylor, 1993). Practically all of them attribute the success, and what is even more disconcerting, even the invention of the little watch to

---

* Extract from R. Carrera following the international meeting organized in Bienne to celebrate the 50th billion Swatch (*L'Express*, 23/9/1985). Elmar Mock was not present and was never invited to an event organized by the Swatch Group concerning the watch of the same name.

N. Hayek.[*] These case studies are characterized by two strong ideas: First, they focus mainly on the history of the product once on the market. And so it is the success achieved by the marketing that is analyzed—world distribution, constant relaunching of the design, consumer craze, fashion item. . . , and, second, they substantiate the idea of a vision inspired by a great leader who imagined a future innovation and who had it made by engineers and competent marketing people. This sort of analysis will flatter any future high-flying manager's ego who already imagines himself influencing the course of business life thanks to his inventive genius. But it does not stand up to the test of the real facts!

The Swatch Group communicated an official list of 54 names of the "inventors of the Swatch" (Trueb, 2010), taken from the inventory of "fathers and godfathers" of the small watch that is to be found in *Swatchissimo* (Carrera, 1991, p. 14). This reference book makes the distinction between "the main actors of the project" (E. Thomke, J. Müller, and E. Mock, along with M. Schmid and her companion B. Müller, as stylists[†]) and F. Sprecher, for the marketing concept (M. Imgrüth was left out). This list of 54 names does not contain the name of N. Hayek. Hayek even admitted in a letter dated April 10, 2008, to Lucien Trueb that he is not the father of the Swatch, following an article that L. Trueb, journalist and expert in the watchmaking industry—who followed the Swatch[‡] project from the beginning of the 1980s—had just published in the famous daily newspaper *Neue Zürcher Zeitung*, April 6, 2008, where he recounts the unofficial story of the Swatch. In his reply, N. Hayek, after having clearly written "[O]ne thing is really sure: I did not invent

---

[*] It is important to differentiate between the case studies that use the official versions (e.g., Gabarro and Zehnder, 1994; Moon, 2004), and those that are based on serous research findings (Tushman and Radov, 2000) that are associated with important figures in the design of the Swatch [e.g., C. Pinson worked with F. Sprecher (Pinson and Kimball, 1987)].

[†] These two people were responsible for the iconography of *Swatchissimo*.

[‡] L. Trueb was lucky enough to follow the story of the Swatch innovation as editor in charge of the science–technology column of the *NZZ* from the beginning the European launching of the watch on March 1, 1983, in Zürich. Moreover, the next day, March 2, 1983, the *NZZ* published a large cover story about the inventors of the Swatch, with a detailed article on the invention of the watch (Müller and Mock, 1983).

the Swatch" (Trueb, 2010), he reworked the theory of collective responsibility, which meant that there were a lot of people who played important parts. The head of communications of the Swatch Group, who was contacted during the preparation of this book, in February 2011, confirmed that N. Hayek was not the inventor of the watch Swatch and made reference to a book of interviews between N. Hayek and Bartu Friedemann. In this autobiographic book, N. Hayek mentions that he was behind the launching of the Swatch (Hayek, 2006, p. 92) and that he had supported the project, while dealing with the upper management of ASUAG and the banks. He situated the technical origins of the Swatch in the 52 pieces of the Delirium Tremens, which has absolutely nothing to do with the structure of the Swatch (Hayek, op. cit., p. 89). N. Hayek took over the SMH in 1986, when the Swatch had already been on the market since 1983, and E. Thomke continued to direct the company for another 5 years. At this time, "opposite E. Thomke who was captain of the SMH ship, the boss Nicolas Hayek was only the skipper."[*]

Collective imagination had turned N. Hayek into the father of the Swatch[†]. . . and he let it happen, making the most of this incredible ambiguity. "The success of a small group of pioneers fired up the pride of a whole nation. It was the greed of the Swatch Group that confiscated the memory of it. From now on the father of the Swatch was called Nicolas Hayek. The myth organized itself around the group and its commercial strategy. The exceptional achievement started to look like a teleology. There was no break, only an unstoppable movement towards the apotheosis of an invention *via* the visionary audacity of a boss, who was at the same time a guru and the CEO. Elmar Mock and E. Thomke had already left the company. Jacques Müller still appeared on the organization charts but was also ejected from the official story" (Danesi, 2005). A lot of revolutions are reappropriated, but they did take place, and that is what is important. It is also essential to remain revolutionary when the situation requires it or when we want to set down the rules.

---

[*] *Le Pays*, 01/04/1992.
[†] We have found a reference mentioning the fact that the Swatch is the result of "a design signed Ernst Thomke [sic] Jacques Müller and Elmar Mock of the [company] Hayek Engineering" (Fiell and Fiell, 2006, p. 474).

2.5.13 The Subtle Link between Creativity and Knowledge

The Swatch story demonstrates how no design is possible without any K's, but if you only have K's, all you can do is reproduce something. Innovation also requires creativity: How do you write music if you cannot play an instrument? You need knowledge in order to be a solo artist, even if being a virtuoso does not boil down just to knowledge, associated with an unbridled, surprising, and unknown kind of creativity. How can a virtuoso take the risk of composing something new after having played the music of the masters for so many years? How do you go about taking the risk of the "creative plunge"? No innovation space is ever closed, even those that are filled by people who have been the leaders therein for a very long time, along with their solutions that work. At the time of the Swatch, the audience (the customers) was used to listening to Swiss watchmakers play classical music. E. Mock and J. Müller offered them jazz, and against all expectations, the public got up and started to dance.

Chapter 3

C-K: A Truly Practical Theory of Breakthrough Innovation

In management literature, innovation leans on two long-standing traditions. The first is psychological and refers to analogy, intuition, improvisation, imagination, and metaphors; to crazy, uncertain ideas; and to concepts. In this case, innovation is associated with creativity and with mental states of creative individuals, with organizations and tools that provide and allow the emergence of innovative concepts and objects with renewed identities. The second tradition is that of science and knowledge. Contrary to the first one, its goal is to ensure the conformity of objects, to stabilize them and guarantee their reproductibility. And so there are "creative people" on the conceptual side and "scientists" on the knowledge side. There are "creative organizations" and "regulated ones." These two traditions have always co-existed without their interfacing or connecting with one another—in other words, the reconciling of concept with knowledge has nothing to do with intuition or spontaneity. And that is why it is necessary to formalize this intertwining and C-K Theory; a rigorous way of reasoning does exactly that.

3.1 Reconciling Concept with Knowledge

To explain and organize the process of innovation, the reconciliation of these two traditions is therefore vital. The Swatch was a dream but it was also engineering. How do you move forward among unbridled creativity and rational know-how? How do you "break" from and go beyond basic *brainstorming* methods that end up locking creativity up in the same space as concepts? How do you avoid the pitfalls of technologists who design intelligent objects that are not very practical and will never sell? To innovate radically, it is essential to work out what makes the breakthrough in both concept and knowledge *simultaneously*.

Innovation is not only putting forth our knowledge with the hope of standing out from the crowd. Innovation wants to broaden and develop a new form of knowledge. It is neither, as is the case with certain creativity methods, the inventory of intuition nor of brilliant ideas that will naturally lead to something simply because you have gathered enough intelligent and astute people around the table. The act of innovating or of designing implies the capacity to think in a space of concepts and in another one—that of knowledge (Hatchuel and Weil, 2003)—at the same time. The designers go from a situation where, when confronted with formulated concepts, their knowledge is not enough to make something out of them, to a situation where new knowledge emerges that creates something and is able to transform the initial concepts by adding qualities to them and even making something out of them as well. This linking together of concept and knowledge is what is required to reveal the unknown and to modify the identity of the known objects. Creativity and knowledge work together: The more of a poet we are, the more of a scientific researcher we will have to become and vice versa. To innovate, it is important to stop having ideas (concepts) and knowledge like everyone else!

So, how do you go about reconciling the conceptual with the know-how? To answer this question we will use the framework of C-K Theory developed at the *Ecole des mines de Paris* (*MINES ParisTech*). In 1994, at the initiative of Professors Armand Hatchuel and Benoît Weil, the *centre de gestion scientifique des MINES ParisTech* structured a collective research and teaching program about the management of design activities. Later on, Pascal Masson joined the project and contributed to its dynamics. C-K Theory is one of the most well-known and innovative results of this program (Hatchuel and Weil, 1999, 2002, 2003). Publications and course material given at *MINES ParisTech* on breakthrough innovation,

"Theory and Methods of Breakthrough Innovation,"* will be used throughout this book.

3.2 A First Approach of the Notion of Design

All forms of society design. The term design is associated with different traditions in art, architecture, and engineering, and it still remains rather enigmatic. It has a vague theoretical status, linked to a long-standing variety of usages that results in the absence of one unified theoretical representation of the concept. We will start by drawing up some general definitions and then illustrate them with a few examples:

- Design is a process intent on obtaining a result that does not yet exist.
- The design process starts with a dream and ends up with the concrete realization of something. The Nobel Prize winner Herbert Simon (2004, p. 201) wrote about this in a reference book about the sciences of the artificial: "[H]e who imagines some measures to be taken in order to change an existing situation into a better one is a designer."
- Designing is related to activity and to thinking, going from unknown objects to known ones.
- If an object does not exist at the beginning of a thinking method and emerges during this method, then this is design reasoning.
- The design of an object is not a description of its properties (since it is necessary to create new ones).
- "To make Aladdin's magical flying carpet" requires a lot of design, since the concept of a flying carpet is defined in the realm of the imagination and that the knowledge needed to create it is not *a priori* available.
- "To build a car for 2,000 euros" requires not only design, but also the rethinking of the whole system of value for the automobile compared to what we already know and may force us to go as far as redefining what a car is.

---

* Launched in January 2009 at the *centre de gestion scientifique des MINES ParisTech* (http://www.cgs.ensmp.fr/design/).

A design starts with the wish to create a new object that is partially or totally different from what already exists. It is neither a perfect copy nor a simple deduction of the previous know-how. It does not necessarily make a clean sweep of what already exists as it tries, as with the case of the Swatch, to reuse existing knowledge.

In management, a successful design is able to produce innovation that spreads in a market or in a community. The innovation is then judged afterwards (i.e., once on the market), corresponding to the result of the design and the values of the people using it. The success of the design is the innovation! In this case, and since this book looks upon innovation as a form of activity, let us go on to clarify a few things (see Table 3-1).

To understand what design is, it is important to look at the theory behind it and to confront it with decision theory before examining the basic notions of the C-K Theory. In order to be practical, we put

---

Table 3-1 The Shift from Innovation to Design

Management papers on innovation discuss two postures regarding the use of the term "innovation." The first is almost incantatory: "Innovate!" It takes the position of the imperative—of an order or a formal demand. On the whole, it inhibits criticism and breeds the fear of not being innovative, of not being up to the innovation challenge. Many a managerial or political speech that encourages innovation postulates that it is possible, but without explaining how it can be done. In support of the incantations, we often find examples of successful innovators or innovations.

The second posture is the realization that defines the innovation retrospectively. The properties of an innovative object are thereby described afterwards. In this case, innovation is either a result (I innovated and it worked, or not), or an appraisal or a perception (anything is innovative when it is considered as such by the adopting entity: the company, group, or individual).

Whatever the posture, the innovation word is a trap for all of us. Indeed, it refers back to a judgment of an object that is already conceived in order to talk about the innovative activity that is underway. But if innovation is defined as a watchword or an observed novelty, what does "I innovate" mean (Le Masson, 2008)?

As mentioned in the first chapter of this book, it is not the notion of innovation but the activity of innovation that is of interest to us—that is to say, all design activity that can lead to innovation. Innovation is a result (nonsystematic) of the design activity. Under certain conditions, after the different traditions of design (architectural, artistic, engineering, management), the activity of design acquires a reasoning, an organization, and performance criteria that make innovation possible. Paradoxically, design is not addressed that much in business studies, but more so in the tradition of decision theories, despite the fact that it is not a tradition of innovation!

forward examples and a methodology of the implementation of break-through innovation.

3.3 The Theoretical Roots of the Design: Design versus Decision

The term "design" does not belong to classic science, unlike the term "decision." To understand the notion of design on a theoretical level, it is important to start with decision models (David, 2002). The latter relies on a procedure of selection of programming and optimizing that emerges out of a repertory of possible solutions. The tools that are thus created, such as operational research or strategic planning, are well adapted to objects and to repetitive projects able to mobilize known and mastered resources, along with well-founded knowledge. On the other hand, they are not very appropriate, being even somewhat counterproductive, when the projects demand highly innovative, creative, and exploratory content. Restarting from the roots of decision theory allows for a good under-standing of this "shift" that is required of design.

3.3.1 The Rule and the Object

A decision model relies on the relation between, on the one hand, a cer-tain amount of knowledge that remains constant throughout the design process and which includes functions, rules, and selection criteria, and, on the other hand, the objects upon which the decision is based. In other words, in a decision model, the function or the selection criteria is iden-tified along with the object that applies to the rule. For example, if you choose "an even number between 1 and 3" we know what the object is (we know what a number is), and the rule allows us to differentiate between even and odd. There is no design involved here, just a decision where we know *ex ante* the rule (often after having searched for it in a repertory of learned rules), but not yet the object (the result). The decision is not only the procedure that uses the rule but also the result of this procedure. If we have to choose "the right film for a Saturday night in with our friends," we have to make a decision which involves using selection criteria that corresponds to the characteristics of the films and to the wishes and the constraints of the friends, along with the relationship between the two.

You have to make a list of the films based on this information and in a limited space—even if this space could be as huge as a town like Paris. Here again, there is nothing to be designed. The decision made does not change the definition of what a film is, whereas if we have to choose to make our own film for ourselves one evening with our friends, the situation would be very different. In the same way, if you have to "find a party that will entertain all the guests," even though we are familiar with the notion of what a party is, we will end up thinking about the definition of a party that might change the idea. Starting with known proposals about parties (a home party with a list of electronic music, a party in a night club) if we involve the future guests in the concept, something surprising and unknown could emerge from this thinking about the party and might end up with *in fine* varied and astonishing proposals (Hatchuel and Weil, 2003). Finally, if you have to plan a trip for 15,000 euros for people during a fortnight, there is nothing to be conceived, only a decision to be made in relation to the criteria or taste concerning the offers (in this case an extensive one). On the other hand, imagine a trip for 150 euros for four during a fortnight—even the idea of a journey has to be thought about as well as the definition of the journey itself in order to design "something else"—for example, an inner journey.

3.3.2 In Order to Design, Get Out of the Rapport "Problem/Solution"

With decision theory, you don't create any objects, you choose them, joining them together and optimizing them with known rules. And so, according to this theory, you determine the choice (a choice among known alternatives), the *programming* (a building of the space of solutions starting from known rules of selection), and the *optimization* (a decision about what is the best solution among a group of specific acceptable solutions). Since the 1950s, the tools for investment choices have developed the means that influence our manner of decision making and our methods of arriving at the decision.

Designing means rising above the decision models that start the thinking process with "taking into consideration all the acceptable solutions, let us use the rules of choice in order to find the right answer in the middle of this entity." To make a decision means thinking in the same space that gathers together the initial questions and the solutions that will solve them. When you conceive a new idea, the problem has no solution, or rather the "solution" is not to be found in an established knowledge base but in the design itself. If there is an object that did not exist from the start, and if it emerges during a thinking process, then we are in a mode of thinking about the design. To get into this mode, we must get out of the relation "problem/solution," something quite difficult for us Westerners, who are educated to make decisions. Indeed this relation is a false lead for breakthrough innovation. Decision thinking excludes all surprises, whereas thinking about design seeks them out, prepares them, and even creates them. Designing an object means regenerating its definition, which requires at least one principle—that of the undecidability of the object. The starting point of thinking about design is the following: An object exists with undecidable properties, but we are unable to produce that product with the knowledge we already possess. This creates a problem that cannot be solved in the space of known knowledge. Designing is not the act of starting from a group of solutions with the aim of solving the problem, but rather starting with the undecided knowledge concerning that given object. The design work consists of getting rid of this undecidability. And it is here that C-K Theory intervenes, proposing an answer that can structure the relationship between the two disjointed spaces, that of concept and that of knowledge.

In fine, anticipating certain definitions that will be presented later on, it is already possible to synthesize the opposition between decision models and design models by using opposite and comparable features (see Table 3-2).

3.4 The Basic Notions of C-K Theory

C-K Theory can be defined with four basic notions: expansion, partition, concept, and knowledge. This theory allows the design process to formalize by a coming and going between the two different spaces—the one of concept (C) and the one of knowledge (K) (see Table 3-3).

3.4.1 The Notion of Expansion

At the same time familiar and enigmatic, expansion pushes back the boundaries of a known space. If it were not for expansion, design would

Table 3-2 Decision versus Design

Decision Model	Design Model
Exploitation	Exploration
From known to known	From unknown to known
Problem/solution relation	Concept/knowledge relation
Restrictive partition or decomposing of a problem	Expansive partition or the extension of a problem
Stable knowledge base with restrictive partitions (see later on)	Nonfinite knowledge base as a starting point with expansive partitions (see later on)
Knowledge of objects and reasonings = we can choose, program, optimize	Revise the properties of known objects or create new objects = we must design
Uncertain	Unknown
Will my street be busy tomorrow? I know my street and its use; it's the frequency that I ignore	Is there life on Mars? If we take this question seriously (or at least the concept that "there is life on Mars"), then the life forms there are different from ours. The definition of life is thus transformed and enables us to imagine new forms of existence
When a car manufacturer chooses to launch a new combustion model to replace an existing line	When someone who is not necessarily a car manufacturer designs an electric vehicle and does not simply electrify an existing combustion vehicle. He imagines new forms of mobility
Choosing a material from a known list	Creating new material
Making a flatter, lighter, and less-expensive wristwatch	Making a watch that is not a watch, with new hitherto unknown properties

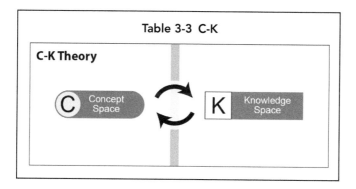

Table 3-3 C-K

be limited to the selecting of items from a list of objects or rules—that is, decision. The expansive identity of an object is its capacity to possess other characteristics than those commonly known. Expansion is at the same time exploratory (exploration is a process that consists of discovering something that exists but is not yet known) and creative (using reasoning to find unknown concepts, knowledge, or objects). And so, triggering an expansion means breaking with a known rule or state. The notion of expansion is used to characterize the notion of partition.

3.4.2 The Notion of Partition

Partition is a simple operation of division* within a design approach. There are two types of partition:

– *Restrictive partition:* This involves the division of a finite space according to the selection criteria or known rules. For example, it is easy to partition the space of films that are showing this week in New York or in London: All you have to do is take the complete list and apply the selection criteria (genres, length, actors, theaters). Decision models have developed and distributed restrictive partition tools. It is a question of separating and assessing what has been

---

* We can also partition by including or, for example, by joining two separate "things" into one (water with earth gives mud): The partition by division separates into clear subsets something that was defined from the very beginning.

dissociated in order to select, *in fine*, the optimal branch of the ultimate alternative (see Herbert Simon, 1947's problem solving).[*] If we take the example of chess, often used by Herbert Simon, the game is confined to an immense space of countable solutions. Simon's reasoning does not consist in analyzing all the possible moves in order to reach a decision, but rather in selecting the best strategies by eliminating the worst ones. It is the SEP decision method (separation and evaluation)/IDC method (Intelligence, Design, Choice). In chess, the objects and the rules are known and do not change during the course of the game. Restrictive partitioning does not change the definition of what has been divided at the start. It rationalizes a given space, albeit huge, by dividing it in accordance with a decision-making process. Simon was looking for a general structure for problem solving. Ultimately, he imagined a machine that could make optimal decisions and thereby win every time.

- *Expansive partition:* This gradually builds something "new" within the space at the start. It adds on new properties, raises new questions, and defines categories—"things" that did not exist at the start of the thinking process. Expansive partitions can, therefore, trigger some incredibly new surprises in relation to the initial concept. If we reuse the example of the "party that makes guests happy," the organizers slowly modify the definition of what a party is and they help increase the number of possibilities at each stage of their thinking. Every one of the possible parties that have been defined are expansive partitions. First of all, we imagined throwing a party on a boat on the Seine river, and then we ended up suggesting having a fancy dress party on an island (Hatchuel and Weil, 2002). As seen with the case of the Swatch, the C of irreparability surfaced during the design reasoning. It did not appear in the first technical *brief.* If we have to organize a journey for four people for a month for 15,000 euros, nothing has to be designed; you just go out and choose what is offered, for example, in a travel catalogue. This is restrictive partitioning. If you have to organize the same journey for 1,500 euros, this is also a restrictive partition, but choosing from the low-cost sector. However, if you have to organize this "journey" for 150 euros, you have to come up with "something else." You have to define

---

[*] Simon H., *Les Sciences de l'artificiel*, Gallimard, 2004, p. 201.

the characteristics of this innovation by using something different, something not to be found in the traditional packages. These defining characteristics will be gradually specified in this chapter. For example an "inner journey" or a "journey that generates income" would be expansive partitions of the initial C.

3.4.3 The Notion of Knowledge (referred to hereafter as K)

K's are propositions that have a logical status for the designer or the person for whom the design is made. Logical means that we can say whether a K is true or false, if it works or not. Logical implies that a K can be evaluated by itself by the experts of K, generally as members of a legitimate community. Behind the basics of Knowledge are a lot of skilled professional people with a lot of work experience. These experts possess the criteria to prove K but also to reveal its truths. K's are validated or can be validated. In other words, the space of K's contains proposals that the designer will consider as established. They are known "things." As such, they can be used in order to act upon "unknown" things. A K confers the designer with the capacity of legitimate action.

From the design perspective, all forms of truths are K's: objects, rules, facts, values, science, techniques, judgements, aesthetics, legal rules. . . . K's must be understood in the broadest sense: there are K's about our clients, on how you pitch a tent, make a micro-chip, dissipate kinetic energy, weld wood. There are K's in the New York Stock Exchange, they may concern your personal reputation, a business model, or an illness such as Alzheimer's Disease. . . . It is important not to limit them to a simple set of scientific or technical K's. Breakthrough design requires all available forms of truths and proof. K's can also be tacit. They are defined by their action, just like logical propositions. At the beginning of a design process the K's are either:

- **Known:** They exist within the organization or within a broad community of designers.
- **Unknown/known:** They exist, but outside the designers' network; in other words, they exist elsewhere and the designers are aware of this, but they do not have these K's *ex ante*. Therefore, they need to

find them outside of their professional perimeter, sometimes very far away, in unexpected places, and yet in accordance with learning processes that can take time.
- **Unknown:** The K's need to be designed.

K is not fixed and is defined in the here and now. It gradually changes during the design process until it "fits" with the concepts that, in turn, will also evolve.

3.4.4 The Notion of Concept (referred to hereafter as C)

C's are new proposals to base the design work on. It is not possible to choose them at the beginning of the design approach. In other words, the C space is a place where proposals have no logical status in K. This means that when a C is formulated, it is impossible to prove *a priori* that it is true or false in K. And so C is not known with regard to the designers' K's. For example "a car without wheels" or a "chair without legs" are two C's, since we do not know *a priori* how to define them in K—but we will know, *a posteriori*, at the end of the design approach. Without any logical status, these propositions are neither true nor false. C refers to the definition of the designers and the architects, to the engineer's sketches, to the designer's briefs, which are understood as the initial proposals of the future object (product, service, organization, space, process). C, therefore, is not a well-defined notion, but on the contrary, it is a notion in progress, it is a possible, potential one. C's open up the design space. By formulating C's, designers allow themselves to think, to imagine and to dream! These C's are sought after unknowns—attractive, infinite by definition, that is, incalculable. And because they are reserved for the C space, they are neither immediately subjected to the dogma of established K's, nor can they be influenced by the market. C-K therefore paves the way for creativity by defining the C's separately (see Table 3-4).

C's allow you to work on what is intangible, virtual, or potential, disregarding *ex ante* the criteria of technical feasibility or pre-existing market analyses. Because it is impossible to have one single definition for any given C by trying, for example, to make an exhaustive list of its properties, and because it is impossible *a priori* to confine the definition

---

Table 3-4 Some Examples of Concepts

A blue sitting room, a green pair of skis, a flying boat, a car that travels at 400km/h (different from "a car that drives faster"), an intelligent supermarket trolley, breaking on wet leaves without blocking the wheels, a cordless phone, Internet in the car, a mobile flat, a telephone for a young adult, delivering hydrogen to secluded areas without any tarmacked roads, a hard disk ten times smaller, a watch 10 times cheaper, the price of Wi-Fi, intelligent glasses, recharging batteries on the move, a self-inflating tent, a bagless vacuum cleaner, an electric car, finding a way to avoid hitting your fingers when you are nailing, a flying carpet or whale.

---

of a C, we can admit that theoretically there is a definite "refusal of the axiom of choice."[*]

Without any logical status, C's are proposals that we cannot say, at the start of the design process, whether they are true or false, whether we like them or not. A C must, therefore, not be *a priori* judged, assessed, or appreciated. This is a fundamental point and puts a stop to the natural and spontaneous tendency of humans to pass judgement when confronted with a disturbing idea:

"That's totally impossible, it will never work!" "I hate it!" "What a load of rubbish!" "I don't believe in it!" At the start of the design approach, critical judgement is kept on hold. Therefore, it is not possible to evaluate a C straightaway. For example, the question is not if you are for or against something, for example, "Internet in the car," or whether you believe in it or not. It is more a case of starting to work in the K space in order to confirm the C, change it, or even stop the design. In the case of the Swatch, we saw to what extent E. Thomke, the Director of ETA, took the initial C0 (initial concept) of the watch "Vulgaris" very seriously, whereas everyone else was rejecting it and referring to it as heresy. Working on a

---

[*] Design theory relies on mathematical set theory. If we have not developed these aspects, it is because the mathematical vocabulary overflows with the notion of the axiom of choice. Simply put, the axiom of choice means that you can ordain a whole that is not empty. For example, acceptable solutions to a problem cannot be described or counted *a priori*. What this teaches us is that in breakthrough innovation, the concept space is unlimited [nor I the K space (what is known), at least in theory]. Hence, we can let our hair down in the definition of expansive properties!

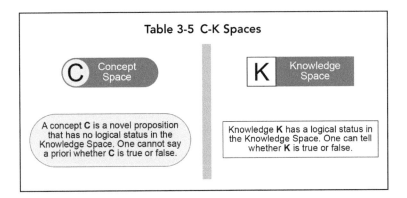

Table 3-5 C-K Spaces

C means waving judgment and gradually specifying the C by adding properties after "detours" in the K space (see Table 3-5).

A C is always "K relative"—that is, it must be comprehensible in K, even if K does not clarify C *ex ante*. In other words, the C space contains proposals that do not belong to the same space as the designer's K's, but they can be interpreted with the K's. For example, a "pink bicycle" is a C that is well defined with the K's regarding paint. A "flying bicycle" (C) is not false from the K perspective with regards to flying. However, a "zero-energy bicycle" (C) is false from the K perspective, except if the bicycle is a static object on display in a museum. . . .

3.4.5 The Concept of Wetness

Wetness can be defined as the capacity of a surface to be wet. It questions how a liquid (we will use the example of water) is brought to and then spread over a surface. It questions the efficiency of the distribution. What must you design to ensure that 100% of the water distributed will be useful for a wash? How do we wet ourselves when using water in our daily domestic life in civilized countries? Can we wet ourselves with less water? With these questions in mind and with a few facts to help (e.g., a typical American uses, on average, twelve litres of water per minute when he showers), let us think about how to find the right terms for what we know and what we are looking for. Functional analysis puts a lot of importance on vocabulary and the means of expression. It is also vital in design reasoning, which uses a lot of analogies, metaphors, and even oxymorons. Let us take the case of the shower: What happens when we wet ourselves? We spray, soak, and bathe as if we were under a waterfall. Although it's unfortunate about all the wasted water, it's somewhat excessive to go to a waterfall just to get wet! So how do we use what we really need—no more, no less? In the wild, we can wet ourselves without going under a waterfall: Mist wets us just as much as the watery fallout of a waterfall or a geyser. Wetness is watering oneself, bathing, soaking, but it is also spraying. The Icelandic mist wets us a lot but with very little water, as it is the huge amount of droplets that create the feeling of "wetness." For the designers who spin these metaphors, the question is now: "How do you wet yourself as if you were in this mist?" At this stage, in order to move ahead, you have to go back to K and work, for example with the K's of the Space Industry, which atomizes droplets in order to launch its rockets, or with the pharmaceutical industry, which optimizes the taking of liquid medication. In other words, you have to find the K's you need for the C of wetness elsewhere. In pushing the design to its limits, Creaholic created Joulia, a shower that uses ten times less water and which not only saves water but also energy by recuperating the heat of the water that comes out in order to heat the water coming in. Creaholic has developed a "high-speed sprayer of hot water" and, thereby, invented Gjosa, a shower that is not really a shower any more. . . .

3.5 The Reasoning Behind the C-K Theory

Armed with the aforementioned definitions, it is time to go into more detail about breakthrough innovation reasoning. The design starts off from a proposition to be solved, called "C," which cannot be solved in the current state of "K." From the beginning of a design reasoning, "C" is comprehensible in K, but without there being an answer or without a clear answer in this space. In other words, C is partly or completely unknown related to the K space. This initial "gap" between C and K is called "disjunction" (Hatchuel and Weil, 2003). On the other hand, when the design reasoning allows C to find the K that enables it to happen then this is a case of "conjunction."

3.5.1 Disjunction and Conjunction

The design process starts when someone wants to describe an object (in C) whose possible existence is uncertain due to the current state of K's.

From a practical perspective, this is what happens when one is confronted with a "brief"—an idea or an incomplete list of technical specifications. At the start of a design approach, the proposal of C has no (logical) status in K. The design process consists of shifting from a desired state (C) to the concrete existence of this state (with K allowing the creation of C). The C's of "a car without wheels" or "a chair without legs" combine two terms that, individually, are well known, but whose semantic combination lends an unknown status to C within K. *A priori* we are not familiar with this kind of object! This is definitely a case of disjunction! At the end of the design process, if the K's have produced C's we can speak of "conjunction": A car without wheels and a legless chair do exist. The design process is complete: The initial proposition, which was uncertain *ex ante*, possesses, *ex post facto*, properties that can be described. C has been confirmed in K.

The design process, therefore, consists of an interaction between the C space, which gradually becomes more apparent, and the K space that develops concomitantly. C's challenge/produce K's that in return challenge/produce C's. The cycle consists of a back-and-forth movement. In other words, the C's highlight the shortcomings in the K's of the different players who explore them and trigger the development of

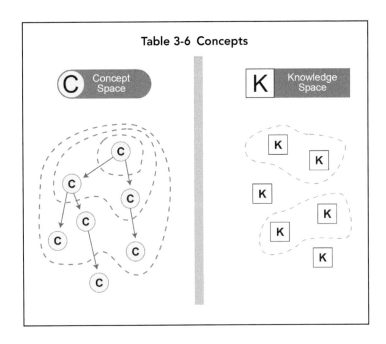

Table 3-6 Concepts

new K's that, in return, question the C's, which can then be extended to new partitions.

The partitions of C can be expansive (addition of a new property) or restrictive, if the new property already belongs to another C that has been partitioned. The K's are explored in pockets that can remain independent from each other. We saw in the case of the Swatch how two pockets of K were shaped in regard to the process and one pocket of K regarding the product (see Table 3-6).

3.5.2 The Operators of the Breakthrough Design or the Design Square

Any design process must be represented by a joint expansion of C and K according to interdependent initiatives or "operators" whose interactions are represented in a design square (see Tables 3-7 and 3-8). These operators refer to the different "mental states" (see Chapter 4).

3.6 C-K in Action: Some Examples of C-K Cases

We will turn to three simple examples to explain the design approach of breakthrough innovation, along with two cases that stem out of Creaholic activities. We will then present the KCP methodology that relies on the reasoning behind C-K Theory in order to make it available to companies and consultants.

3.6.1 Designing a Flying Boat

Starting with an initial C (C0), "a flying boat," the terms that define this proposal are comprehensible but do not have a known status in K (Hatchuel and Weil, 2002). Even so, the basis of K is not void in terms of its relation with C. Concerning the flight, the designers can for example mobilize the K's on the wings and propellers which they may use to go back to the C space in order to partition it. But the partition of C0 in a "boat that flies without wings or propellers (and which is not a hydroplane, since we are looking for something unknown)" is an expansive

Table 3-7 The Design Square (Hatchuel and Weil, 2003) shows the 4 C-K Interaction Operators

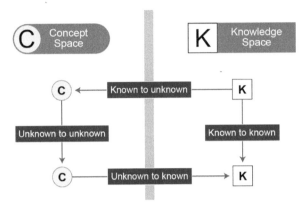

The first Operator, "Known to Known." Properties of concept **C** are modified by the influence of knowledge **K**.

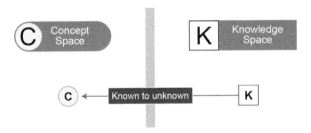

The second operator, "Unknown to Known." This operator gives a logical status to concept **C**. When knowledge **K** already exists, it serves to validate or invalidate **C**. When **K** does not already exist, opening a knowledge gap or disjunction, new **K**'s are developed in response. In practice, this corresponds to validation tools or to traditional design methods, such as the consulting of experts, running tests, conducting experiments, or building a prototype. A completed design (conjunction) is reached when a sufficient number of propositions from **C** can be determined as true or false by **K**.

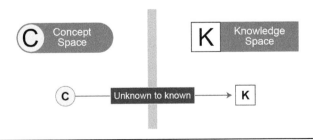

(Continued from previous page)

The third operator, "Unknown to Unknown." Here, designers create new concepts **C** from existing **C**'s. This typically occurs during creativity or brainstorming sessions, where ideas are bounced around. These expansions are purely conceptual and are common in artistic design.

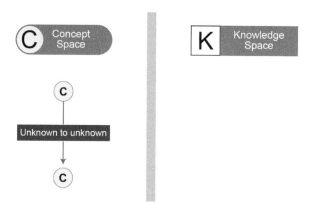

The fourth operator, "Known to Known," transforms known propositions into known propositions, without ever using unknown propositions. This operator corresponds to the production **K** based on an existing **K** (auto-expansion of the **K** space). R&D researchers and scientists master this form of method of the production of **K**.

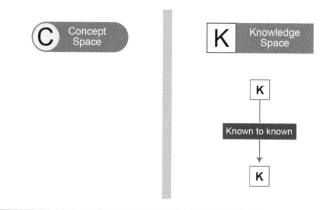

partition. This then forces us to go back to the expansive K space in search of *a priori* surprising K's (Table 3-9).

What flies without wings and propellers? The designers will have to define the K of hot-air balloons, kites, airships, or flying fish. By increasing one's knowledge of K's about the flying fish, it is not a case of

Table 3-8 An Example of a K → C Operator: The Concept of the Banshees in Avatar

In *Avatar*, a film by James Cameron that was released in 2009, the concept of the Banshees, flying creatures of 36 feet in length, is an excellent example of a design job, where the unknown is made out of something known. It is important to recall that J. Cameron and his teams designed an entire universe for this film, an imaginary planet called Pandora.

Banshees don't exist, and have never existed, and yet we have the distinct impression that we have already come across them (see the notion of the oxymoron). This creature is at the same time familiar and strangely new because of its characteristics. How did Cameron and his designers go about designing them? The initial concept defined by the producer was a mixture of a dragon and a Pterodactyl (known), but Cameron wanted *in fine* an animal that differs from what we normally see in science-fiction films (unknown). Starting with this familiar concept, the teams of the film pushed it to the unknown by making an in-depth detour by the **K** space.

"The artists enriched their imagination with the contact with the real world. They spent hours watching documentaries about bats in order to see how the membrane of their wings were articulated . . . The most difficult part was . . . getting familiar with the unfamiliar, in such a way that the spectator does not lose ground and yet at the same time making him discover a totally new unknown animal" (Duncan and Fitzpatrick, 2010, p. 23). The design of the Banshees required much more work than any other animal on the imaginary planet of Avatar. Here, the **C** space is progressively modified, partitioned by the **K**'s: The unknown (**C**) is created from the known (**K**).

Table 3-9 The Flying Boat

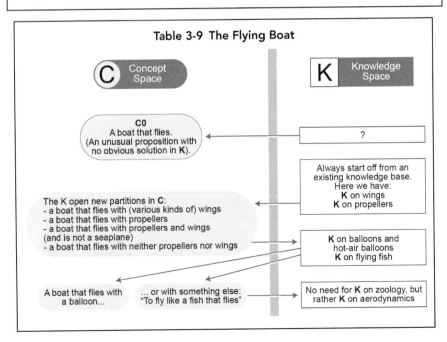

Figure 3-1   The Hydropter.

designers turning into ethnologists but a question of obtaining a better K base of animal aerodynamics. To prepare to glide, a flying fish swims very rapidly near the surface of the water, with its fins touching the sides of its body. When it leaves the water, it spreads its wings without flapping and its speed increases. It uses its rear fin as a hydrofoil or as a point of contact in order to prolong its glided flight. In possession of these K's, the designers are now ready to define "the hydrofoil craft," a boat that flies on some foils that offer minimum points of contact, thus eliminating the inertia of a boat hull (Figure 3-1).

Between two strong waves, the boat flies. The conjunction that results is an object with new characteristics. The design work is finished.

3.6.2 How to Design an Innovative Camping Chair*

If we start with the following C0: "Design an ultra-light camping chair that does not take up a lot of space, is easy to put away, is very inexpensive, has an acceptable amount of comfort, and is not yet on the market,"

---

* As with the previous example, this one was thought up for teaching purposes at MINES ParisTech.

the uncertain part is in the "light" and the "inexpensive," and in the unknown that is claimed (not yet on the market). Of course, if someone shows you a camping chair that is in compliance with C or says, "Impossible!" then the design is dead. The K's that we possess force us to project onto the C what we already know, that is to say, we create a different chair but in restrictive partitions, like the famous history of the design of chairs which is an eternal "rebeginning." However, if the C0 is taken seriously, it can end up producing an awesome result. Starting from the K space, we will find a lot of known proposals: K's concerning the price of chairs, their uses, the volume, the materials, the balance in a seated position, the distribution systems, the marketing. . . .

In particular, the K's about the "balance in a seated position" are generic and will hold the attention of the designers. In other words, since it is a question of redefining the traditional identity of a chair, let's start by looking at what is at the heart of this identity: A chair has four legs (which allow the feet of the sitter to touch the ground) and a back to support the spine. With our new K, we can go back to the C space and partition the C0 into a "camping chair with four legs," "three legs," "two legs," "one leg." These partitions are restrictive because they clarify the C in relation to K, which already exists and which has already engendered a large quantity of chairs. There is the example of the chair with a single telescopic leg for photographers or fishermen, helping them to move around easily and without losing the comfort of a sitting-room chair. If we push this partition about legs to its extreme, the chair with no legs appears. At first, this C seems quite surprising, idiotic, and without a future, but it is still necessary to take it seriously. This part of the C0 of a "legless chair" is expansive as it adds an unknown characteristic. To progress in the reasoning at the level of this partition, an operator C-C would be very useful by making a distinction between "with the human" or "without the human," that is to say, by partitioning the C according to whether the human is involved or not. This sort of criteria is often used in designer workshops when a human is absent—an object can come and fill the space (Table 3-10).

The C "zero leg chair balanced by man and object" leads the designers in K to an expansion that consists of, by trial and error, finding K, which then allows C to be found. A result of this breakthrough innovation is the belt (Figure 3-2).

For example, the Chairless of the Vitra Company is a belt that has been commercialized, 55-cm long and 5-cm wide making a buckle that,

Table 3-10 C-K for a Camping Chair with No Legs

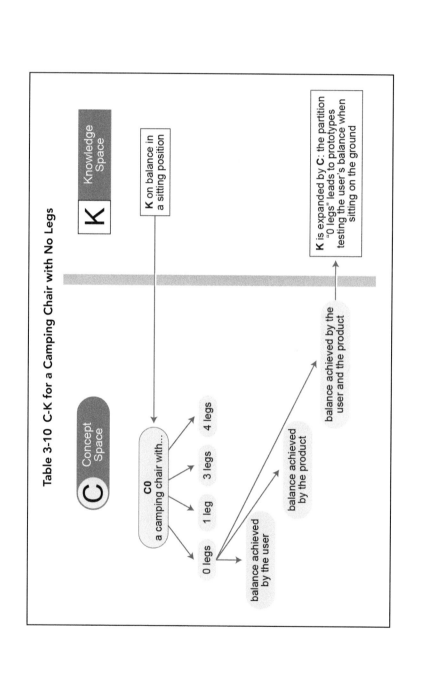

Figure 3-2 The Sitting-Belt.

attached around the back and the knees, creates a sufficiently stable seated position. Such a belt is easily carried. Weighing only 85 g, this band, folded in a very compact way, can be kept in the pocket of your cloth-ing—an ideal emergency chair away from home. Chairless is, therefore, an alternative to the chair: Chairless is a seating accessory destined for contemporary nomads. This robust band of material enables you to be perfectly seated in a back-less chair, which makes it the perfect solution when you don't have a chair: for a picnic in the park, for an overcrowded airport waiting room, during a concert, for reading on the beach, and for a variety of other occasions. Chairless is so light and compact that you can take it with you everywhere. Chairless relieves pressure from the backbone and the legs:It is no longer necessary to lean against something or to push your knees against yourself. This multiple relief creates a feel-ing of overall relaxation for the whole body. That way both of your hands are free: to use your lap-top computer or your iPpod, to read, or to eat, etc. (Adapted from www.architonic.com/pmsht/chairless-vitra/110355).*

---

* In reality, this belt was not designed using the C-K Theory, which is used here *a posteriori*, as a rationalization. However, Chairless takes its inspiration "from a belt-chair" used by the Ayoreo Indians. This nomadic ethnic group lives in the border area between Paraguay and Bolivia and has always used ribbons of similar textiles to stay in a seated position. It is the Chilean architect Alejandro Aravera who discovered it (http://www.architonic.com/fr/pmsht/chairless-vitra/1103553; accessed in August 2011). In fact, we do not

This type of belt seems at first quite strange, as it emerges from a traditional definition of the chair, of what a traditional chair is commonly thought to be. The notion of *dominant design* is a prohibitive one! Chairmakers may know their products well and, therefore, all the restrictive partitions that are involved, but do they know "the chairspace?"

Haven't chairmakers ever studied the concept of "sitting down on the ground?" And so, if we start thinking in this way, we end up with the following options:

- Learn the lotus position, or try to sell a handbook describing, "How to learn how to sit."
- Study the "prothesis" that helps increase the comfort of a handicapped person when she or he sits on the ground.
- Design the Chairless.

A company may know its products but does not necessarily know that C's enable you to find the solution. To transcend what exists and to master K's is disconcerting, and that is exactly what innovation is!

3.6.3 Moving Around with One's Suitcase

Let's imagine a design team in a suitcase factory that wants to innovate from the concept C0 "driving with one's suitcase." When there is an abundance of objects, the design space seems very closed. We must approach C in its broadest sense, which means not only looking at the suitcase of today (defining C in terms of a "wheel suitcase"), but also attempting to work out how you can move with your suitcase by fixing it to an object that moves (car, bike, motorcycle). The work is thus focused on the design of an interface between the suitcase and the moving object. However, the approach we have been following until now always starts with a double partition in C of a traditional suitcase.

---

know if this Indian inspiration is true but let's insist on the fact that once innovation has occurred, it is often reinstated in a pseudo line or genealogy of the product in order to justify or to commercially legitimize its existence. (e.g., The Indians, before Chairless; the Delirium Tremens, before the Swatch). These genealogies speak to the consumer, for they are reassuring and avoid any mention of the Innovation Factory.

We have seen in the previous example how a classic partition key in C-K consists of making a distinction "with" or "without" the involvement of a human (often the user). Moving with "one's suitcase without a person" leads to, for example, the design team creating a "K" based on remote control systems that allow for the suitcase to be driven by short waves via a mobile telephone or by any equivalent user system. The suitcase thus moves around on its own next to its owner. This attractive design is however very expensive. In contrast, in the case where we use a human being, the team can imagine a prototype of a "wheel suitcase," that does not only have advantages when used, for example, tidying up in a circle or being able to climb stairs. The team also works from the expansion C → C between the involvement of a human being "next to the suitcase" (the current known market method that focuses the attention of innovations) or "on the suitcase." This second branch of the partition is the expansive adding on of a new characteristic to what is already known. But, at this stage, there is a disjunction between "moving with a human on the suitcase" and the K's of the professional world, which is made up of "moving with the man next to the suitcase." The expansive partition leads the team to mobilize K's (they already exist but are remote) concerning

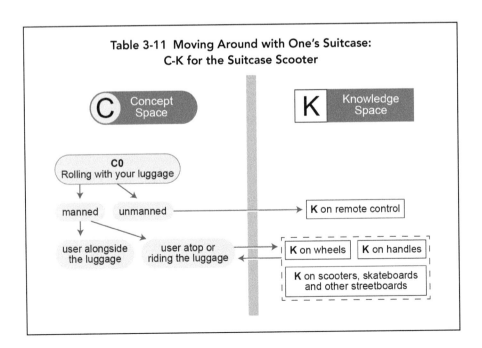

Table 3-11 Moving Around with One's Suitcase:
C-K for the Suitcase Scooter

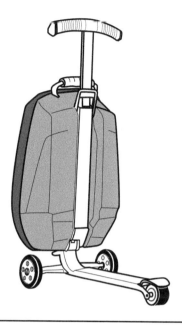

Figure 3-3   Moving with one's suitcase.

urban glides (skates, ice skates, scooters) and to focus on the fixing system and the articulation of the suitcase and these different kinds of sliding (see Table 3-11).

At the start of the design process, nothing suggested that the team was going to test skateboards or other forms of urban sliding, such as scooters and design scooter-suitcases or suitcase-scooters. A product is already on the market, the suitcase-scooter, whose hybrid and renewed identity not only offers new forms of mobility but is an excellent way of getting noticed (Figure 3-3).

3.6.4 Re-asking Forgotten Questions: From Welding Wood to Welding Bone

The treatment of wood has remained the same for centuries, and we have been fixing wood in the same way for the last 500 years. To cut a long story short, Stradivarius used the same technologies as IKEA today! Why can't you weld wood? When the company Creaholic presented this concept for the first time, it was rejected: "What's the point? It's not possible; we only weld steel." Indeed, for a very long time the question of welding wood was asked but always put aside because it was a "non-question." It is as simple as this: It's absolutely impossible. However, if we take this concept seriously it could open up a large design space with the known and the unknown.

Contrary to the "tunnel" creativity method that eliminates all bad ideas one by one in favor of the good ones, the designers seek to enrich their K base and thus open up the design space. Logically, if the K space is closed when you realize that the art of welding steel cannot be applied to wood, it is nevertheless important to open up the K's of welding, to put aside traditional definitions and question what is known and what is ignored in other methods of assembling wood and thus proceed "as if" it were welded. It is with these new K's in our possession that we can go to the C space and clarify or displace the notion of "welding." Why can't we weld wood? The designers have set up a K base starting from an observation of "what works" in its natural state. And so, the tree is neither screwed, nor riveted, nor nailed, nor embedded, nor glued, and yet it stands up. The roots work like fractal and intimate liaisons that do not seem very strong if taken individually, but as a whole they are very resistant.

The K's of the roots lead to an expansive partition of the initial C in the shape of C: "fractal liaison." This C is an oxymoron since it expresses the possibility to "weld without welding." In other words, the designers, using welding as the starting point, keep the principle of a solid liaison, "as if it were soldered," but without turning to what the common K's consider as welding. With this new C of "fractal liaison" in mind, the design continues with a return to K. At this point, Creaholic will reuse a K that it mastered to perfection ever since the days of the design of the Swatch watch. It is, in fact, the welding technology of plastic by ultrasound that will enable the design to progress. After numerous trials, Creaholic developed a pin or an injected plastic element that is integrated within the porous fibers of the wood. The horn transmits mechanical energy in the form of oscillations to the thermoplastic element, which then heats up. Once it has liquified at the interface, this element then filters into the porous material. The plastic cools down in a few seconds and welds everything. And so two pieces of wood can be assembled together by this interface with a thermoplastic material and create a unique whole that is extremely resistant and long lasting (Figure 3-4).

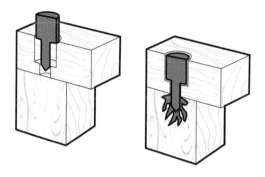

Figure 3-4   Welding wood.

This device makes the "welding" of the wood possible, along with its industrialization. For example, the furniture industry can use it as an alternative that is cheaper and stronger than the traditional solutions, such as fixing with nails, screws, or other forms of glue. WoodWelding SA is a spin-off company of Creaholic, founded in July 1999, which commercializes a wood-welding procedure.

Why don't we go a step further: Can we weld anything else apart from wood? Can the technique work with other porous materials that are capable of supporting a certain amount of pressure? Nothing *a priori* seems to be an obstacle to proceeding with this design approach. Many tests are carried out. Can the technique also be used on living porous elements? From wood to a living organism is just a step away, which the designers were able to take after numerous trials. The characteristics of bone are similar to that of wood, but when we work on a human-related issue, the system closes in and hurdles to be overcome are huge because it is necessary to obtain the health authorities' approval in order to go to market. The C "welding bone" is born out of the intellectual challenge of an agitator factor and of WoodWelding SA, which received the Swiss KTI Medtech Award 2005 for its project entailing the development of medical applications from its technology, in collaboration with the Maurice Müller Institute at Bern and with the University of Zürich. Up until now, more than 15,000 surgical operations have taken place. Table 3-12 shows the design approach.

Breakthrough innovation consists of not going in the same direction as everyone else. The design that obtains results has to prove that the impossible is possible.

Table 3-12 C-K for Woodwelding

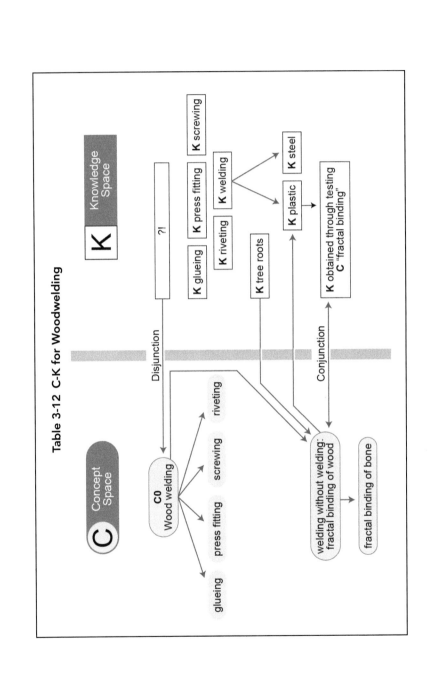

3.6.5 Consuming Ten Times Less Water When You Wash Your Hands or Designing a Tap That Is No Longer a Tap

At the beginning of 2000, Creaholic had already accumulated more than twenty years experience in caps and closers in the food world. This market is well organized around big packaging companies, such as Tetra Pak. Here the innovations happen step by step: cheaper, stronger, lighter, easier to use when opening or closing. It was while working on a project for a client in the food field in 2003 that a breakthrough innovation was to happen. Creaholic was working on innovative functions for caps to be able to dose in a precise, hygienic, and repetitive manner. While working for a client on this type of design, Creaholic was forced to develop a strategy of "rights outside the domain." This strategy consisted of getting the rights to use the spillovers of an innovation developed for one client patented in a completely different field of activity, without competitive overlaying. Here, Creaholic obtained the rights from its client to pursue breakthrough design work on the measuring cap, outside the food world.

At the beginning of the reasoning process, there are simple and fundamental questions to be asked: How do you economize rare resources? How do you avoid wasting what is precious? How do you find an alternative: do without or waste? Without any study or particular data, the designers of Creaholic came to the following conclusions: Today, roughly a third of the world population does not have access to enough "drinking water." The demographic increase that concentrates itself in the cities increases the need for hygiene, which creates a higher sensitivity to the presence of bacteria. The planet's reserve of drinking water is diminishing faster than it can be regenerated. In this context, How do we use the water resources more intelligently? How do we economize without going without? How does a "clever dosing cap" allow us to deal with this paradoxical problem?

3.6.6 Wash Better and Rinse Better

The pursuit of design starts from the observation of common habits. Let us think about having a shampoo under the shower, or a hand wash. Nowadays (for those who are lucky enough to have access to a water network), you wash your hair or your hands and then you take the shampoo

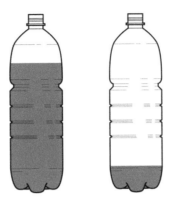

Figure 3-5   Usual water consumption when washing one's hands versus consumption when using Smixin.

or the soap and you mix them with the water that stays on your hair or on your hands, you rub, and then you rinse. In fact, soap on its own does not wash, it only helps the water to remove the germs and the dirt. It is only the mixture "water/soap" that washes efficiently. But we have the tendency to use too much soap. Finally, when you think about "rinsing one's hands," you are rinsing the leftovers of the soap on the skin, and this elimination of the concentrated soap uses much more water. When you wash your hands, you run a lot of water for nothing, because only a minimal amount of water is effectively used for the washing. We have no idea of the amount of water we use in order to wash our hands: between 0.5 and 1.5 litres for each wash. Under these conditions, the system that should be designed should optimize the dosing of the soap and diffuse a mix of "soap, water, and air"; you must obtain/produce soapy frothy water that wets well, washes, and rinses better. This entails a huge breakthrough design that would lead Creaholic to develop a system that would allow you to wash your hands using ten times less water: You can wash your hands perfectly with half a glass of water. This innovation was completed and transferred to its spin-off, Smixin, in December 2009 (www.smixin. com) (Figure 3-5).

3.6.7 Revolution Instead of Renovation

The innovators of Creaholic did not improve the tap, which is what the other established competitors had as a strategy; they created a new

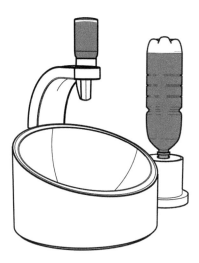

Figure 3-6   Prototype of Smixin unit.

category of product by modifying the physical, functional, and sensorial relationship between water, air, and soap. Their design comprises the properties of both a "homogeneous mixture" and a technical system of an "intelligent dosing-mixer."

The demonstrator used by Smixin (Figure 3-6) is made up of a reservoir of soap in the upper part, a water inlet, and an instantaneous mixing system just above the hands of the user. This mixture is soapy frothy water, the result of difficult design work that relies on the pockets of K that Creaholic possesses and masters.

The system works in three phases:

1. A captor detects the presence of the hands, and the system delivers a mixture of soap, water, and air.
2. During a pause, the user washes his hands as long as he likes.
3. Finally a cycle of clean water provides an efficient rinse that uses very little water since there is no need to eliminate soapy residues (Figure 3-7).

3.6.8 Design the Sensorial

The designers at Smixin worked on the design of this object with the intention of emphasizing the ecological commitment that says that "here"

Figure 3-7   Washing hands with Smixin.

the way you wash your hands is totally different from anyone else. Anglo-Saxons speak of products that are "nice to have." Ostentation is always a part of the success of the innovation: The design of the "tap" must be very pure and use high-quality products that are also very durable. The desired design has to be timeless, futuristic, and yet seem familiar. The feel of the object and of what it diffuses has to be soft and pleasant, relaxing and tempered. The sense of smell should also awaken memories and projects of a known world. Finally, sound is almost absent, reduced to the noise of the flowing water, creating a feeling of calm. And so it is not enough to patent a mixing system from a K using the mechanics of fluids. You also have to design the conditions that make the device emblematic and agreeable to use (Figure 3-8).

Figure 3-8   An autonomous, mobile Smixin unit.

3.6.9 The C-K Reasoning behind Smixin

With this innovation, the target was not to ration but to do things in a different way. It is not a question of using less but of using more intelligently, while continuing what was done before. The designed device is a fertile and reassuring oxymoron; it reassures because it innovates in continuity. The designers reuse the known and mastered K's (minimalist use of design resources). Continuity is also what provides the points of reference to the user, who is not totally thrown off by the innovation: It looks like a tap, there is a sink, and it washes your hands "as usual" (see Table 3-13).

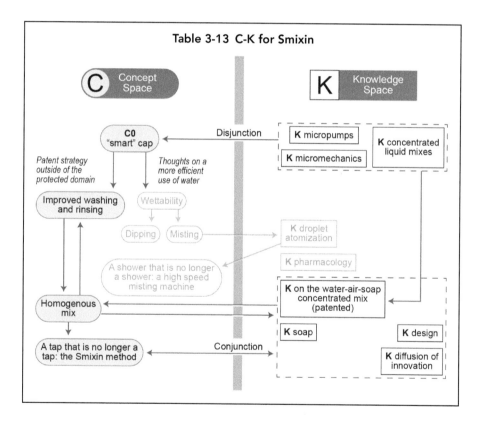

Table 3-13 C-K for Smixin

3.6.10 C-K in Practice: The KCP© Method

C-K is a clear example of an efficient design process. A useful and obvious use of C-K is to redraw, time after time, a design process. But is this theory enough to control and to manage the Innovation Factory? We will not start to discuss this here (Choulier et al., 2010), but simply assume that C-K is not only a reasoning framework—a means of representing the design—but it is also a tool for action in design.

There is indeed a methodology called KCP, which helps the design that relies on the C-K Theory (Hatchuel, Le Masson, and Weil, 2009; Elmquist and Segrestin, 2009). KCP is a collective breakthrough innovation method developed by the *Ecole des mines de Paris* (*MINES ParisTech*), along with its industrial partners. It allows us to develop a breakthrough design process, while benefiting from the know-how derived from so many jobs and partners, thereby including and associating new uses, economic models, and technologies in an original manner. The KCP design workshops bring together from 20 to 40 people. In 2008, this method became a "company method" at the RATP [Régie autonome des transports parisiens (Parisian public transport)], and a good number of large companies (Thales, Sagem, Vallourec, Turbomeca, Areva, Moveo, Volvo, etc.) also use it. The method comprises three phases:

1 - The *K phase* organizes itself in collective sessions in order to create and share a K base. This phase is not at all creative but busies itself with the integration of K, that is to say, it aims to share K's in order to prepare the "return to the C" or the emergence of new C's. No creative effort is needed, and any hasty searching for solutions is discouraged. The K phase is based on the idea that in order to collectively draft new C's, you must first of all have shared varied and numerous K's that, at the same time, confirm the obsolescence of the solutions currently applied, bringing out new potentials for development. The more of a K base we have, the better we can work with the C's. In the words of Rudyard Kipling, "He who knows only England, does not know England." This is the phase in which all sorts of job backgrounds come in handy, and it might even be necessary to outsource (e.g., clients or suppliers). With regard to the creativity methods, the C's are used as a starting point for the research of K and not as a single endogenous expansion, that is to say reduced to the C space itself (C → C) . The task of reviewing the K's is vast and not restrictive: It can be K of the user, relating to the company's strategy or to the status of techno-scientific art, phenomenology, sociology. . . . The K phase can include a genealogical dimension

that retraces the transformations of the objects by the K's. If this phase looks like the collecting of information, it is different from a traditional state of the art because it will also be concerned with the census of "non-art." A great number of works and methodologies in creativity refer to "out of the box thinking," but do not clarify the fact that the K's are out of the box. A KCP workshop will put forward a state of the art and a state of non-art. The K phase is not only the sum of K's in the possession of the participants of this workshop. The state of non-art will help to provoke and to make the breakthrough of C by answering the question, "What don't we know?" This problem reveals the weaknesses and limits in the K retained by the company and also consists of the paradoxical, ambiguous, polysemical, strange, and audacious dimension that will facilitate the innovative return to C. The case of WoodWelding SA showed that if we did not know how to weld wood, it was nevertheless possible to learn how to do "as if," that is to say, to create a K base on welding what is not normally welded. In a large field of exploration (in this case, welding wood), we find K's that traditionally define the terms and enclose them in known solutions. The non-art pushes the exploration of the K's to the limits of the field. Apart from the traditional K's of welding, what knowledge do we have that allows us to weld, giving us the same result as the classic art? The K phase is, therefore, not only an inventory of regulated and stable proposals, but it clarifies the multiple meanings and approaches of K for the existing objects and the future objects to be designed.

2 - The *C phase* starts off the act of creativity under the direction of the workshop leader. This phase does not intend to produce a great number of ideas, as is the case with a lot of creativity methods, but it hopes to create original and divergent C's (in the sense of expansive partitions). The group, which has already created its K base, is divided into sub-groups and must work from initial C's. Each group has to explore a C and propose solutions (K) that are appropriate or define the missing K's. Throughout the process, the designers keep in mind (until the emergence of all the expansive partitions) all the K's they already have and consider irrelevant. We will see with the example of Smixin (Chapter 5) how the K's that derive from the dosing of coffee machines or ice dispensers can validate a C with a "system that allows you to wash your hands using 10 times less

water." The groups also define the K's that are missing and thereby deduce the main directions for any research (return to K). During the C phase, the groups present their results to each other, helping to reinforce the creative power of the group. The K pockets are reused from one group to another. This means that each group does not design its own solution but, instead, combines and shares the partitions that it obtains. Finally, in contrast to the brainstorming of creative methods, which seek the freedom to diverge, the C phase manages the addition of properties to the initial C.

3 - The *P phase* (P for projects) must allow for the carrying out of an accumulation of work and the concrete development of original proposals that come out of the C phase: prototypes, models, new products or services, search for new partners, research programs. . . . The breakthrough innovation strategy that is a result of KCP cannot be reduced to simple ideas of products or services, but has to define a coordinated and structured program of immediate action (e.g., using solutions with existing K's on a C original), mid-term actions (validating a semi-product or a prototype with potential users), and more long-term actions (e.g., acquiring new K's thanks to research programs). It is a shared agenda of innovation that is set up, defining many original alternatives and preparing the breakthrough. The top-end management of the companies are involved in this phase. The P phase prepares them for innovation by giving them reliable information and by making them ascertain what has already been learned and what remains to be learned.

3.7 Conclusion: The Origins of the Concept

The C does not just simply appear out of the blue. It can be coerced by the environment, as in the case of the Swatch where the little cheap plastic watch was a riposte to the Japanese attack. The C can also come from the designers themselves, from their creativity or their K's. The quality of a design resides in large part in the definition of the C0 or the original concept. But it is not always enough to have a creativity meeting to define it. We can provide two solutions to this problem, the first is in the form of an oxymoron, and the second is presented as a metaphor.

3.7.1 The Concept Defined by an Oxymoron

An oxymoron is a stylistic figure of speech that combines two terms, generally a noun and an adjective, which appear to be opposite in meaning (e.g., an eloquent silence, a virtual reality, a light obscurity, a dark sun, a sweet and sour sauce, a silent ringing. a cold flame, a horrible pleasure, giant dwarves, feathered fish, etc.). The oxymoron opens up the space for the description of a situation, of a person, or of a concept. By creating a new reality, the oxymoron accentuates the unexpected, the surprise, the absurd, and the unbearable. It is widely used by certain authors who want to innovate with words. The French poet Arthur Rimbaud is an emblematic figure who frequently exploited the brilliant effect of the oxymoron. His "Illuminations" are evocative for those who are interested in innovation.*

We saw to what extent the oxymoron provided fertile ground in the case of the Swatch, wherein the C's had to be formulated, so much so that it opened up the design concept instead of just improving on what already existed. The oxymoron reunites the unknown characteristics with the known ones: a watch is no longer a watch, a chair is no longer a chair, a tap is no longer a tap. The radicalism of innovation resides in this capacity to preserve the known characteristics of the objects and yet is able revise the known identities! (See Tables 3-14 and 3-15.)

3.7.2 Distorting Oneself without Distorting Oneself

Using a technical brief of a paradoxical design as the starting point, a famous German car manufacturer and a very big German steel consortium told Creaholic: "[W]e want to innovate the design of the steering column of cars in order to reconcile the extreme rigidity of the column while we are driving and its softening when a shock happens in order to protect the passenger compartment." What distorts without distorting?

---

* A good example: "ecstasy during the destruction" (Conte), the "disintegration of the climax" (Villes 1), "scientific fairytale" (Angoisse), "soft eruptions" (Promontoire), or "marvelous reason" (Génie). US equivalent: Emily Dickinson/Walt Whitman/Alan Ginsburg.

Table 3-14 A Breakthrough Design Approach

"Frying Without Frying": A Breakthrough Design Approach That Was Born Out of an Oxymoron Concept (Chapel, 1999)

Vincent Chapel participated in a breakthrough design for the French company SEB. He helped SEB find a "solution to how to reduce the smells of fry-ups." The initial problem was simple: The frying of food causes unpleasant smells for our noses, and the odors tend to linger for a certain period of time. So what has to be done to reduce or be rid of this inconvenience? V. Chapel explained the problem of SEB in the form of a **C** oxymoron for he believed that the problem was how about "frying without frying"? In other words, it is essential to design a system that, for the French-fries consumer, does not change the taste but reduces or eliminates the nasty smells of the fry-up. Starting with this deliberately paradoxical proposal, the designers explored the **K** field, from the (1) food point of view; (2) from the cooking side; and (3) from the gas emissions perspective.

1. In order to eat fried food without frying it, we could first externalize the frying function and use food that has already been fried (such as oven French fries), or we could eat fried food away from home. Today, two-thirds of the consumers of French fries eat them away from home, and the company could move its business model of deep fat fryers to the sale of French fries.
2. We could also imagine alternative ways of cooking, such as steam cooking, which achieves more or less the same sort of results.
3. We could try and get rid of or reduce the smells by working on the quality of the oil or the treatment of the gaseous flow. Concerning the gaseous flux, the **K** experts differentiate three possibilities: capture, elimination, or transformation. Capturing the gaseous flux has already been done with different sorts of active carbon filters, but this idea has been rapidly put aside as it creates performance problems over a long period of time.

Likewise, the elimination of the gaseous flow is too complex to be adopted for products of mass distribution. The other option is the transformation of the gaseous flow by three different identified procedures: washing, photocatalysis, and a catalysis system taken from the car industry. It is this last **K** that is finally adopted and brought to SEB by the car industry. The product that eventually arises out of the design is the Azura Purair SEB©, a successful innovation of the brand.

What are the analogies at the start of the breakthrough design reasoning? The phallus or the tin can may not seem like very serious subjects to use during meetings with important industrial clients. But these are some of the paths to be explored by them alongside Creaholic . . . a phallus or a tin can is rigid when it is full, and supple when it is empty. Can you imagine a

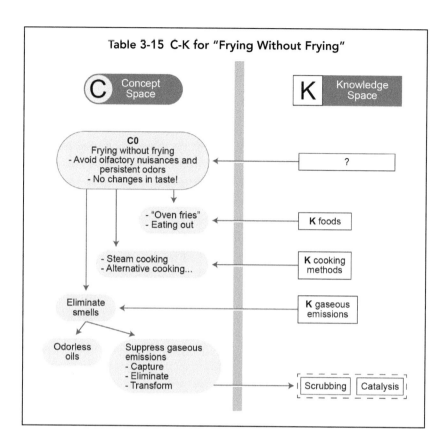

Table 3-15 C-K for "Frying Without Frying"

steering column that contains a liquid that is released in five milliseconds in case of shock, which allows the column to be distorted straight away? In this case, we no longer only work on the characteristics of steel (this is the strong but focusing point for the steelmaker) but also on the redefinition of what a steering column is. Parallel to a design, the Creaholic teams organize "seminars" with the client to deconstruct and reconstruct the initial question. Along the way, Creaholic will shake up the client by bypassing established models and safeguard systems. The oxymoron is, by definition, an invitation to travel.

3.7.3 The Metaphor of the Pearl

Oysters make pearls naturally when they are protecting themselves against a disturbing factor. When a foreign body slides into them (or is introduced), they secrete mother of pearl around it, making it smooth and inoffensive. This metaphor shows how innovation is there to solve a problem, to make life easier, to confront any disturbance. And so, in order to innovate, you must first find the disturbing factor. Innovation is to society what a pearl is to an oyster. And we also know how to organize our social life around what disturbs us. We know how to adapt to difficulties; we deal with stuff, and we do not always want to change our habits. Often, to change means to suffer, so why do we go into the unknown when we can stay in the known? To find the pearl, you have to overcome these habits and face the disruptions that surround us, including those that we have not even begun to think about.

Creativity as a definition of innovative C's is a particular way of isolating disturbing factors that surround us and finding permanent solutions that allows for them to be eliminated. This requires an essential capacity to destroy objects—"creative destruction"—in keeping with the famous saying of Joseph Schumpeter. Forever dissatisfied, the creator seeks revolution, not only renovation of what already exists. The big difficulty for the creator is the incredible capacity that human societies have of putting up with things that disturb or of simply being happy with half solutions. They like to work on symptoms without tackling the real problems. And so, human society accepts mediocrity, because it is scared to change, to diverge, to break the rules, and to design.

When a company designs "a self-assembling tent," it faces two different groups of use—habits of clients and of established distributors and providers. Indeed, the self-assembly removes the disturbing factor of the assembly of a Canadian tent. The observation of daily habits and how we put up with disturbing factors is a fertile source for C.

Finally, designing causes the expansion of a C and *in fine* makes it happen, thanks to the corresponding K's. In design, there is no real goal to be reached or rather the goal is the capacity for expansion. The objective is known *a posteriori*. The value of the design does not necessarily boil down to a final conjunction of "C" and "K" but also lies in the concepts kept on hold and in the K's created during the thinking process. Throughout the whole of this chapter, the approach was to adopt new K's to break and to renew the identity of known objects in opposition with the traditional thinking of the Western world that began in the 17th century, going from truth to truth, from known to known, from knowledge to knowledge. To innovate, you must work simultaneously in the C and

K spaces and in the area of their interrelation. C-K combines the two logics of creativity and knowledge, and, more often than not, designers, engineers, market researchers, buyers, or financial investors have to work together on the design, thereby adding to the logic of the two spaces. The role of the designers is to produce something unexpected. The formal language of C-K may appear complex, but once it is mastered, it allows for a better understanding of the specificity of the design process.

The next two chapters will examine the conditions required to implement breakthrough innovation: organizational requirements in Chapter 5 and psychological ones in Chapter 4. Elmar Mock, who had to deal with a period of downheartedness following the Swatch. Indeed, the innovator's blues is a natural part of what most designers experience. A period of sadness at the end of a project is quite common and raises the question, How do you get back on your feet? In fact, signs of innovation foment in these periods of difficult transition, and they could lead to a coherent system of breakthrough innovation.

Chapter 4

The Molecular Metaphor of Innovation: Gas, Liquid, Crystal

4.1 The Innovator Blues

At the end of Chapter 1, we left the parents of the successful Swatch in the arms of euphoria at the end of the project. Postpartum blues occurred, as is often the case after certain births, for it is never easy to hand over your project to others. After two years of working "undercover," and after four years of developing the product process, of patent registering, and of picking up the industrial pace, the Swatch became an innovation, a new product on the market, and the designers were naturally less and less in control of their "baby," which was looked after more and more by the same people who were going to exploit and distribute it. Once you have had a taste of what a successful breakthrough innovation feels like and you have been thrilled by the whole experience—at the end of the emotional tour de force—a strange and ambiguous period begins in which you have to take a break in order to recharge your batteries. And, then, a need emerges, the need to "start" to give birth again, to recommence, to relive the adventure of innovation.

"I did not realize to what extent I had spent the last 10 years of my career in a sort of protected cocoon . . . I didn't have to bother with anything administrative, with sales or even public relations. I was able to spend all my time searching for knowledge and solutions, testing in an empirical manner the imagined concepts and exchanging with my colleagues and partners of the company during countless meetings. But the stress I had accumulated during the Swatch and Rockwatch period, along with my hang-ups about the management of what my group* had become, were making me more and more dissatisfied, and I could not see any way out, apart from leaving the company. I was also desperate to discover other industries, other horizons. . . . To become my own boss seemed the only solution. I had the impression that I was trapped," confides E. Mock. In order not to fall apart, he decided to rid himself of the stress by standing on his own two feet. However, the reality of the outside world was very harsh. First of all, nobody was waiting for him. Secondly, the management with whom he had difficulties was the same as the ones on the outside. And even though a lot of people talked about innovation, very few people actually applied it and in a radical manner.

It is fair to say that radical innovation is present in a lot of management speeches, like a "chant," a form of incantation. Advertising messages, political speeches, board or upper management press releases all insist on the need to change, to be a step ahead of the competitors, to even risk breakthrough innovation. Everybody is yelling for innovation, but they make renovation, the incremental supersedes what is radical. We would love to make breakthrough innovation, but we remain firmly in the field of rule-based design. The pressure of the short term by the shareholders (if there are any around), the reduction in resources, the established forms of governance, the bonuses, the career plans, the exaggerated use of risk management, and too much caution prevent us from considering the impossible possible, from designing something that, for the moment, is unknown. On top of everything, any failure to find a

---

* After the Swatch, the group SMH streamlines under the management of N. Hayek, with the introduction of procedures and systematic transversal management systems. The company reorganizes itself in order to rationally exploit the success of the Swatch innovation and in order to integrate the companies and the brands dispersed up until then. It was said, off the record, that the group was crystallizing, which is quite normal at this stage of its evolution.

Table 4-1 The Reasons Why the Influential Big Companies Favor Incremental Innovation Rather Than (Disruptive) Breakthrough Innovation (Christensen, 1997)

The fact that the companies want to serve, first and foremost, the interests of their large and financially viable clients results in their indifference to anything different, thereby leaving the way clear for any competitors to exploit the breakthrough technologies. Indeed, the use of resources is determined according to the wishes of the big clients, who tend to ask more for improvement rather than breakthrough.

The bigger an organization becomes, the more successful it is, the more it needs to have important, established markets in order to maintain its rhythm of growth. The large and influential companies are part of a network (of clients, suppliers, partners) and have internal routines that encourage them to develop incremental innovation. On top of that, middle management of the dominant companies does not even need to try and take risks concerning a situation that has advantages already.

It is thus rational, from the risk-taking point of view, to wait for a market to be ripe before investing in it. And so the large, dominant company has a tendency to neglect the emerging markets, which are inherently smaller, where innovations start to be distributed by avoiding the established offers.

The fear of failure is most real, and when you are dominant and successful, failure is phenomenal.

---

breakthrough solution will have immediate consequences, all losses will be highlighted, and any allies of the concept risk losing their jobs or, *a minima*, the trust that the bosses bestowed in them.

When Clayton Christensen was teaching at the Harvard Business School, he clearly explained the reasons why the large and influential big companies favored renovation more than breakthrough innovation (1997).* He believed that it is not due to a lack of competency but rather because of the internal governance and the relation of the company to the environment, especially when dealing with large clients (see Table 4-1).

How do you get past this contradiction, this double language between innovation and renovation? How do you finalize? How do you go about

---

* According to Christensen, supportive innovators improve the performance of the established products, however, without changing the bearings of the market actors, whereas disruptive innovations add new values to the markets. The supportive technologies improve the existing ones, whereas disruptive innovation transforms the rules of the game by changing the dominant design of the objects.

doing breakthrough innovation? We can handle this topic by using the design approach, as presented in the previous chapter with the C-K Theory, but we can also deal with it in terms of organization and take it a step further in terms of mental states.

The setting up of an *ad hoc* structure or the hiring of a head of innovation is not enough, as an organization is incapable of producing innovation on its own. It is the organization that creates the conditions for the activity of the individuals, either by coercion or by making it possible. All innovation requires a collective action and an organized environment that at least provides the competencies, the social relations, and the necessary resources. *In fine*, the key element is always the human being. It is important that the individuals cooperate, formulate and choose the concepts, and use or develop their own knowledge. The framework is a crutch that supports creative intuition and the use of knowledge but does not have any control over it. If the organization is only a facilitator of the innovative activity, it is necessary to dig deeper into the analysis of this "human factor," which the organization either encourages or inhibits.

We will now examine what we call "the mental states," thanks to the molecular metaphor. Certain mental states can steer us to renovation rather than innovation, and vice versa, as we possess many hidden ways of thinking that are more or less conducive to being innovative.

4.2 The Origins and the Status of the Molecular Metaphor

If we are incapable of changing society on our own, in the short term, at least, we can try to understand why we have such difficulty—especially regarding innovation. Faced with this lack of understanding, it is important to construct one's own analytical grid. And so, in contrast with the C-K Theory presented in the previous chapter, the molecular metaphor was not hatched by a team of researchers but critically tested by their peers. This is how the "used theory"* developed, in order to help achieve

---

* Chris Argyris and Donald Schön (1996), two important specialists in organizational learning, differentiate between the "taught theory," which corresponds to what is said or claims to want to do, and the "usual theory," which, in fact, corresponds to what we do, that is to say, what activity is carried out.

innovation. When E. Mock left the SMH group in 1986, he was under the impression that he was an innovator in a company that was no longer able to innovate. He realized later on that this was not something specific to that company. In situations like this, we are convinced that we are right and that the rest of the world is wrong. It is impossible to have this sort of attitude for very long because we are similar to the person driving on the wrong side of the highway who believes that all the other foolish drivers are going in the wrong direction. The molecular metaphor is first and foremost a "theory" developed by an innovator who has dreams and who wants to understand what he is going through and how he should proceed. Eric von Hippel (1986) said that this is a theory of the "experimental user," developed in order to resolve one's own difficulties, when there are no solutions, no explanations. Elmar Mock had to come up with his own theory to understand what was happening to him and, above all, to help explain it to those with whom he wanted to work. The metaphor positions you with yourself and in order to interact with others. From the start, it is a simplified model that helps one to comprehend the different kinds of analyses and attitudes towards innovation, along with the misunderstandings regarding it. It explains different rational types of behavior and caters to the transcending of value judgments (everyone is a fool apart from myself!), with the aim to understand and learn before being able to go on to become a serial innovator. This theory is at the heart of the creation of Creaholic and has been fortified by 30 years of experience in innovation. It is used for innovation, for the interaction between the innovator and others, and with all others. . . .

4.3 The Molecular Metaphor of the Mental States of Innovation

Is this passion for finding other ways, of being different, this anarchistic need to question established beliefs, this interest for revolution so rare? In fact, the capacity to innovate is a very common gift among humans. Teresa Amabile (1996), a world-recognized expert in the field of creativity and professor at the Harvard Business School, was very clear on the subject: Even if the majority of managers think that only a few hundred people are gifted with creativity, each individual can demonstrate creativity at varying levels. When we are born, a great number of us have a huge creative potential. Individuals who are motivated by their work often behave in a creative manner, but the majority of people do not realize what their creative potential is, partly because they evolve in an environment that destroys any kind of creative motivation. Creativity does not only occur among creative individuals; we are all (boringly) creative!

That being said, where are the adults who have conserved this implacable fizz, the pleasure of designing within the structure of their professional activity? What happened to everybody else? Why is the dialogue so difficult between the creative people and middle management, and why is it complicated for them to get along if we are all so creative? Why is it so hard to innovate, and why do we come across so few breakthrough innovations when so many companies are active on countless markets?

Let us use the metaphor of the water molecule. Be it vapor, drops, or snowflakes, the formula of water remains the same. Only its state of aggregation differs: gas, liquid, or crystal. We humans also experience different mental states. The molecular metaphor helps define and differentiate them in order for us to be able to talk to and understand one another (see Table 4-2).

4.4 The Mental State of Gas

The gas mental state is the mental state of creativity. It is used to describe the mental state of those who create, invent, imagine, expand, share, and dream. Incapable of reducing the gaseous mental state to a strict definition, we can portray it with words that shed light on its multiple facets. Intuition, inspiration, dreaming, freedom, fantasy, imagination, and creativity are often used in order to describe the lighter side of this state

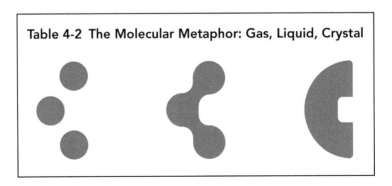

Table 4-2 The Molecular Metaphor: Gas, Liquid, Crystal

Table 4-3 Childlike Thinking or the Art of Being Different

As children, we were good at dreaming and creating and then school started. As young adults, we discovered reality, logic, systems, power, efficacity, and efficiency, the ISO 9000 standards for some of us. All these things slowly mature, becoming points of reference in our society, and all of these are in opposition to creativity. "As a child, a seemingly minor incident probably changed my life forever—I broke my leg in a ski accident," remembers E. Mock. "Break a leg!" In English, this expression brings good luck to an actor before he goes on stage. However, in French, "ça vaut mieux que de se casser une jambe" ("it would have been better to break a leg") has no positive connotation at all. But for E. Mock, this broken leg and the long period of convalescence at the hospital that ensued were a period of isolation and of mental introspection. "I discovered the immense pleasure of daydreaming. . . . My physical and conceptual environment were my field of exploration."

---

of mind. Mirage, chaos, illusion, utopia, reaction, and vanity pertain to its darker side. Nothing is certain or logical in this state. It can either give birth to a monster or to a genius. In this gaseous mental state, you have to, therefore, accept the possibility of a certain form of utopia. You might be taking a huge risk, but, who knows, it might also be the promise of a great revolution.

It is the mental state of a newborn child—of child's play where total freedom, illusion, and the imaginary rule (see Table 4-3). We are familiar with this state as it reminds us of our childhood, but we are not really capable of keeping a lot of these memories alive.

Who is not in awe of the capacity small children have to absorb the world that surrounds them, questioning it and integrating it in their games? But too often we forget that we adults still possess this mental state, similar to a mirage, a hidden potential, or an active state.

The gaseous state is not something that you can use on its own. It is not an end in itself but has to be changed for it to be capitalized on, similar to the emotions of poets invisible to the reader, who share their feelings by transforming their emotions into poetry, accessible to all. When you condense a gas, you change it into a liquid. And yet not all organizations (most are still far from it) are able to create the right conditions for this metamorphosis to occur, and they make do with the lack of creativity associated with the mental state of gas (see Table 4-4).

Table 4-4 The Gaseous State of Mind

Key words: freedom, movement, fantasy, inspiration, dreams, imagination, creativity, utopia, reaction, explosion, chaos, pressure, illusion, intuition, inspiration, expansion, illumination . . .

In the story of the Swatch, the risk that the watch industry might disappear or go bankrupt created a huge stress for the actors, which allowed a gas mental state to blossom and led to the emergence of the unpredictable.

4.5 The Mental State of Liquid

The liquid state is that of apprenticeship, school, development, and transformation. This mental state is the prerogative of all developers and transformers: It is the birthplace of evolution, education, and the criteria of aesthetics, proofs, and truths. In this state, "things" grow and shared facts are built and stabilized.

The liquid state is obtained by fusion or by condensation. Fusion brings to mind the idea of reincarnation, wherein an old idea, an old concept, or an existing piece of knowledge is reborn and resurfaces in a new form. The liquid mental state is characterized by a capacity for mobilizing and redesigning old ideas in order to create new ones, such as in fashion, which provides so many examples of this. As for condensation, it is not the reuse of an old idea but the tangible expression of a new one. Condensation allows us to go directly from utopia to realization. For example, when the iPhone was developed by Apple, before its launch on the market in 2007, it materialized a utopia that was internal to the company. During its commercialization, it was seen as a new product, revising the known identity of a mobile phone. Liquid no longer

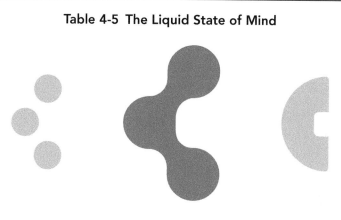

Table 4-5 The Liquid State of Mind

Key words: motion, condensation, fusion, saturation, fluid, softness, grace, evolution, density, tears, sweat . . .

dreams, it makes and transforms. However, in this mental state, things are not definitive; evolution and movement are still possible. This mental state expresses itself in movement, but without too many fits and starts, more in a laminar and regular way than a turbulent one. It has a fluid side. In the liquid phase, a company has rules, as in rule-based design; it has processes, a temporal framework (planning and organization), and an economic framework (aims, business models). However, we must not underestimate the difficulties and even the suffering that this mental state incurs. It entails blood, sweat, and tears, for there are a lot of hurdles to be overcome in transformation. Indeed, it is not because design is based on rules that it is simple! The experiences of our first years in school normally remain firmly anchored in our memory: School marks the change to the liquid mental state. The latter is very present in the organizations that produce the socially legitimate knowledge and expertise, organizations that validate, certify, and guarantee proof and truth (e.g., training institutions, R&D) (see Table 4-5).

4.6 The Mental State of Crystal

The crystalline state is the empire of the rational world, the main reference of our Western society. It is defined by order, rules, stability, seriousness, structure, power, force, maturity, concreteness, operation-ability, and reproductibility. The crystalline mental state often appears as a goal in itself, a quest, a political programme, a proof that we are responsible adults; it is the result of an undertaking that was meant to be initially creative but which has lost all of its quintessence. We have hardly evolved at all from a genetic and physical point of view over the last 5000 years, and our existential fears are identical to those of our predecessors. We still fear tomorrow and are still scared of dying. Knowledge and today's technologies offer us incredible means, along with medication, to calm down our anxiety. A simple example is the calendar: With all the appointments we have made for the next few months, it is totally unthinkable that we could die. The business plans, career plans, retirement, life insurance, budgets, and political programs are projections into the future that try to reassure us and to calm down our visceral fear of the unknown.

Our first experience of the crystalline mental state normally takes place during our professional or academic life, and during our acquisition of musical and handicraft skills, in short, during our entrance into the adult world. This mental state allows us to improve on what already exists and what we know. It is the mental state of always doing better and always making more of the same thing. Every product or service that is successful is structured (in its value chain) in a crystalline way. However, it is not

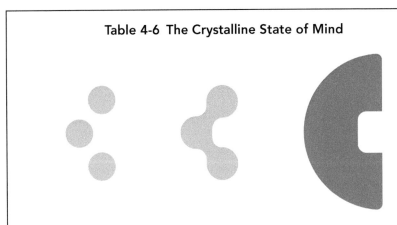

Table 4-6 The Crystalline State of Mind

Key words: logic, systematics, ISO 9000, clarity, standards, routines, rules, control, ability, efficiency, structure, reality, accuracy, seriousness, power, stability, virtuosity, strength, consistency, maturity . . .

by making more candles that we innovate in the world of lighting; we do that by inventing the electric light bulb.

The more order that is present, the more pure the crystal and the more the memory of its origins in the gaseous state are distant. The crystalline organizations guarantee the routines of the cooperation, produce and reproduce the standards and the norms, function according to the hierarchies and in compliance with solid rules, know how to define value, make the specifications, and know the rules of the trade and the criteria of validation and of performance (e.g., the army, the factory). An impressive amount of literature on the theory of organization studies these structures, showing how they have (in breakthrough innovation language) managed to conserve the stability of the identity of the objects (see Table 4-6).

4.7 From a Dialogue of the Deaf to a Dialogue of the Mental States

These three states are very different and are not at all coordinated with one another. Even if they speak the same language, are from the same culture, and have the same education, the dialogue is extremely difficult between two people who are in different mental states, and the situation becomes almost unbearable between the masters of the gas state and those of the crystal one. When the crystal man speaks to the gas man he gets annoyed: "This guy is uncontrollable, chaotic, unreliable; why doesn't he do what I ask him to do? Why does he always propose another idea when he still hasn't finished what he showed me the day before yesterday? He doesn't respect the budget nor keep the deadlines; he should organize himself like me. I pay him to solve problems, not to create them." The other guy is also just as categorical, when the gas guy derides the solid guy: "This guy only sees the money side; he is narrow-minded! He hasn't understood that the world is changing. He is a war behind with his jack-boots! He is headed straight for the wall; each idea I give him is like pearls to a pig." The opposition between the two is deeply rooted and universal, and if it gets nasty, the winner will always be the crystal guy. However, it is not a case of fighting but of interacting, of mutual respect and of being able to work together. These three states are not exclusive and not "definite." They co-exist inside every individual. The strongest is the crystal state, it's the army, and, yet, during times of conflict, there have always been creative generals. We have all experienced these three mental states during childhood and adulthood. A healthy human being will conserve the capacity to go from one to the other, but only in specific daily activities. It is possible for an administrative judge to be passionate about contemporary music during his spare time, or an artist to be happy in the safe haven of his family home, or for a Swiss investment banker to paint non-figuratively over the weekend. It has been demonstrated how, during the design of the Swatch, the engineers became creative, and the designers were trained in process engineering. If the three states are experienced simultaneously, it is fair to say that there is a serious risk of schizophrenia; but the same person can go from one to the other, and people from different mental states can get along. This is what is at stake.

In order to be a "good" mental gaseous-minded person (good in the sense of having the capacity to innovate), it is important to have a crystalline past. Here we can see the lessons learned from the Swatch chapter and from the previous one about the necessary accumulation of an important base of knowledge in order to break the rules of the known. It is necessary to accumulate a lot of virtuosity in K in order to explore innovative C's.

The metaphor serves *a minima* in situating itself in relation to others. What is their mental state? What is mine? The answers to these questions free us from the initial blockage: me against the rest of the world who doesn't understand anything. The mental states are not there to make value judgments, but only to help us to understand the interior conflicts and the frustrations of the innovators in a crystalline world. This metaphor also enlightens us about what makes breakthrough innovation so difficult. The contemporary business world is extremely crystalline, whereas contemporary innovation is directly linked to the gas and liquid states.

The companies that are focused on the crystal state seek to eliminate from their structure the gas state, which is considered to be too deviant (from this point of view, the design of the Swatch is an historical heresy), but they put up with the liquid state because they are conscious of their needs and their usefulness: This is the growth zone of the crystal. On the other hand, a company that is dedicated to breakthrough innovation has to concentrate on the gas state by adding a liquid capacity in order to have an area for exchange and for mutual understanding with its clients or crystallo-liquid partners (see Table 4-7).

To be very practical, this metaphor allowed Elmar Mock to understand his interior conflicts and the frustrations that led him to resign

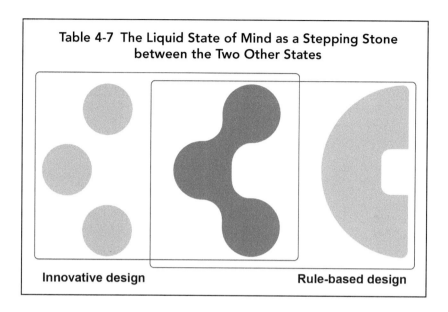

Table 4-7 The Liquid State of Mind as a Stepping Stone between the Two Other States

Innovative design

Rule-based design

from his job in the (future) Swatch Group. It helped him emphasize what makes breakthrough innovation so difficult as well as explain why there is such a small number of inflexible, creative people in the industrial and services world. These thoughts combined with the desire to develop an activity based on repeated breakthrough innovations in many fields, led to the creation, in 1986, of Creaholic. At the very beginning, Elmar Mock worked on his own. After having left ETA, he worked in the evenings and on the weekends as a teacher at the university and in schools. It took him four years to earn enough money to be able to support his family and to be able to employ someone else. At roughly the same period, Elmar Mock met someone who was going to become his first partner. Marcel Aeschlimann had been one of his students and he agreed to join the company without any salary. Since then, Creaholic has developed a great deal and is an organizational model of breakthrough innovation.

Chapter 5

The Metaphor of the Matriarch

5.1 How to Organize Breakthrough Innovation: Creaholic, an Innovation Smith

How does breakthrough innovation actually work? How is it organized? This chapter will examine Creaholic, a company specialized in breakthrough innovation that is also a creative laboratory specialized in the design and the development of new products and of new technologies and their industrialization. The company works on its own projects as well as on those of its clients. The innovation services for multinationals or SME's comprise roughly 80% of Creaholic's activity. The company has roughly 60 main clients. Since it was founded in 1986, it has produced over 750 innovations, filed 180 different families of patents, and created 8 start-ups. The company employs 30 people from different backgrounds and cultures and has forged its own unique specializations. Over the last 30 years, less than 10 colleagues have left this company, which has grown in a progressive and organic manner. The company employs experts from many creative fields: physics, materials (in particular, plastics and wood) in electronics, chemistry, mathematics, law or intellectual property, design, interior design, architecture, economics, and commercial development. Creaholic works from the moment of conception to pre-production, integrating along the way aesthetic values, rules of engineering, construction, research, filing of patents, prototyping, and analysis, as well as the use of materials and appropriate forms. Creaholic comprises a team of people who ignore the boundaries between disciplines, services, and sectors thanks to their transversal manner of working on new subjects. Its work culture is: leave the main roads, propose extraordinary concepts, and feed your creative thought. Because they completely integrate technique and aesthetics and work in small groups with specific tasks, the company is able to help its clients innovate, by developing new concepts and new knowledge.

5.2 Professional Inventors

From the client's point of view, this type of company is a service provider of breakthrough innovation. What it offers to people who are under pressure and going around in circles is a fresh and fun new way of thinking. It also helps them to get started on something. Behind the false fairy tale–like image of nice, young, relaxed innovators are real professional inventors who strictly reconcile creativity, knowledge, agility, rapidity, and efficiency in different fields of innovation. Today, the word innovation has been galvanized to such an extent that it is necessary to define the characteristics of breakthrough innovation companies. They do not simply work on the ideas or the concepts; they also produce and deliver an innovative output. Indeed, this chapter will clarify the positioning of these companies in comparison with engineering offices or BE's (*bureaux d'études*). More globally speaking, these makers of innovation have proven how easily they manage the unknown, that part of the shadow that scares so many established companies. Historically speaking, the immense Thomas Edison Center, built at the beginning of the 20th century in Menlo Park, NJ (USA) and the Thomas Edison National Park, in West Orange, NJ (USA), are incredible representations of varied innovations that were systematic and repeated. The Innovation Factory of Edison worked simultaneously and in incredibly different fields—the perfecting of new technologies, the development of new modes of distribution (e.g., systems of trained salesmen), the design of new industrial systems (e.g., the development and the industrialization of a sound recording system, from its conception to its paid distribution on the Internet) and the design of new client values (e.g., the exploration of new leisure mass markets around sound and image). How do breakthrough innovation factories actually work? How do these professional inventors actually organize themselves?

A rule-based organization does not (any longer) need breakthrough innovation; the pleasure and the joy of inventing is not its motivation. First and foremost, it is essential to conduct the daily business. Creaholic was created and developed according to objectives and a form of governance that is different from any rule-based design. The first aim of Creaholic is to forge concepts with its clients, as well as techniques, designs, products and systems, and business models, in order to give them, *in fine*, a timely and competitive advantage. To survive, it is essential to be able to repeat the innovation process. How do you go about organizing a breakthrough innovation company that constantly prepares for future generations of activity? Does it have to structure the gaseous and liquid states? Does it have to confront the market by creating its own innovations, with the risk of crystallization in the exploitation of a regular and specialized sort of activity?

5.3 Unique Organizational Principles

A few seemingly simple organizational principles that are, however, quite complex have to be implemented in order to allow Creaholic to conserve its coherence over the last 30 years, as well as to reach its company objective of breakthrough innovation.

1. *No production or market sales of the results of its designs.* If the company did this, it would find itself in the situation where it would have to crystallize in order to organize its activities in the field of exploitation rather than in the exploration field: producing, distributing, improving. It is the past developments that structure the organization and not the Innovation Factory.
2. *Never work with the competitors of one's clients*, as making breakthrough innovation is getting to know and learning how to identify the future of its clients. Mutual trust is an indispensable condition for the success of this undertaking. The respect of this principle

obliges Creaholic to constantly look for new territories for products, services, concepts, and knowledge, in which the company is not necessarily recognized *a priori* as a specialist. However, this is how it will be in precisely the best position to support new proposals (the extension of the base of knowledge, K, of the clients!). *De facto* the company works in many sectors—in food, pharmaceutical, automobile, chemical, packaging, watchmaking, etc.

3. As a corollary of the expansion of the territories of activity, the creation of a team must thus be extremely multidisciplinary, while avoiding the danger of too much specialization that could trigger crystallization. The need for growth and the constant instability due to the lack of repetitive projects or of long-term ones (there is no plan of action for more than 3 to 6 months), forces the Creaholic team to find new fields of activity. "We are always on the move," explained one of the managers of the company. This provokes change on a permanent basis, engendering the discovery of new spaces of K. This is not the best way to exploit the acquired K's, the objective of the company, but rather the expansion of those K's. "We are often mistaken for an engineering company or an engineering consulting firm, but our work stops where theirs start," clarifies E. Mock. Creaholic spreads its K's, whereas an engineering consulting firm rationally uses all the K's it has in its possession. And so Creaholic manages to maintain the gas and the liquid together.

4. A traditional structure of hierarchy and capital is counterproductive in breakthrough innovation. Creaholic has searched for a mode of governance that is compatible with creative profiles, even encouraging creativity, and especially ensuring the need for recognition and avoiding a sense of injustice. The directors of Creaholic have thought out their own system of organization as an oxymoron, that of a capitalist kolkhoz. It is characterized by a total transparency within the company on such sensitive matters as everyone's income, bonuses, accounts, or the order book. Another major difference in the governance is to be found in the participation of the capital that is non-transferable and thereby remains compulsorily linked to a specific activity within Creaholic. The following paragraph will explain in more detail this rather unusual setup, which affects the general behavior of the employees. Furthermore, all major decisions are made in compliance with the majority of shareholders who are

present, regardless of who owns the capital shares. The decision process is deliberative—everyone can speak out, exposing and defending his or her point of view. This governance does not aspire to be egalitarian, it wants to be fair and inspiring. Its implementation was made keeping in mind the need to complete the tasks of the company, thereby adapting itself to the instability of its activities.

5. Convinced that you become a better blacksmith by working in the smithy and convinced that Creaholic must refrain from any direct commercialization, the directors of the company decided, during the second half of the 1990s, to develop alongside their role of designer for their clients, an incubator that transforms some of its own company ideas into start-ups. If Creaholic works most of the time for its external clients, the company also produces its own innovations. It is thus necessary to confront oneself with the reality of financing and of the "carrying" of the idea right up to the market. This secondary mission takes up 20% of its work time but also defines and tests the business models. Creaholic start-ups reinforce its credibility in its main field of activity and sets the company apart from other "innovation consultancy" firms. Lastly, it is a vector of communication for the Innovation Factory: "We do for ourselves what we promise to do for you." Creaholic has given birth to companies such as Miniswys SA (which works with micro-engines), WoodWelding SA (which works on welding wood and bone), Smixin SA (which works on the ultra-economical distribution of water for hand washing), and Joulia SA (which deals with green energy). Creaholic has expanded every two years with a new company. Let us recall, back in Chapter 3, through the example of Smixin, that Creaholic developed a strategy of out-of-domain rules with its clients who accept this. Creaholic obtains the rights to use the outputs that result from the innovation developed and patented for its clients in another field of activity, without any competitive overlapping. For example, with a client from the car industry, they would negotiate the possibility of reusing the C's and the K's in a field of innovation that has nothing to do with the car industry.

The company has an annual income of 5 to 6 million Swiss francs. It is not only a gaseous entity able to work for crystalline customers but also a liquid one capable of organizing itself. Apart from the principles and the meta-rules of governance that have just been mentioned, how does such an organization actually work? For the time being, let's focus on Creaholic before opening up the perspective of other sorts of management and of the tension between exploration and exploitation.

5.4 The Internal Organization of Creaholic

The Partners

Everyone who works at Creaholic is a "partner." This choice of words removes all mercantile connotations, not only from the corporate language but also from the working environment. Partners are consulted about every major decision to be made in the company, and they can access all the strategic information thanks to an "open book" philosophy. A partner can also be an investor in a spin-off start-up project. His shares make up the wealth of the partners and not of Creaholic. Every partner can eventually become a shareholder according to his level of "merit." Today, just over a third of the partners are shareholders.

The Shareholders

Only people who work at Creaholic, helping to make it grow, can become shareholders. The capital is only in the hands of the shareholder partners. All external dole outs are impossible, which is not the case for start-ups that develop outside Creaholic. They can open up and out to external investors. The capital cannot be inherited, shared, or sold to non-partners. And so the shareholding reflects the history of the development of Creaholic. The company has combined activity and property in an attempt to avoid all capitalistic behavior of "pensioners" who focus merely on property and who live off the benefits of the assets. The company is valued at a minimum, roughly a third of the annual income. The buying and selling costs of the shares are fixed at the lower end of the scale deliberately limiting the fortune. The increase in value does not stem from the capital but from the innovative activities! Since only active members of Creaholic can be shareholders, excluding all external investment and thanks to the fact that the value of the shares is so low and that Creaholic refuses to work for its client's rivals, only the development of its own activities can thus create value. No pension scheme, no renovation, no repetition can be found here! Under these circumstances, the only way to survive is to be innovative. The sharing of the capital is not an egalitarian one, since a third of the shareholders must own more than two-thirds of the shares in order to preserve the presence of an experienced company core (five shareholders own 90% of the capital). The shareholders, however, decide on an egalitarian rule of "one man, one vote" for all company decisions: contracts, bonuses, pay raises, launching of start-ups, increase of capital, hiring, strategy, investments, partnerships, etc. A shareholder, just like a partner, is also an investor when he decides to allocate funds to a spin-off. This plan of action compensates for the loss of dividends that is due to the fact that Creaholic invests money in its companies instead of handing it out to its colleagues (it is better to be paid by activities rather than by annuities). The profits of the shareholders are obtained with the dividends and the acquisition of spin-offs and not because of the sales of shares. Whenever a shareholder leaves the company, he has to sell his Creaholic shares. The acquisition of shares for a new shareholder depends on the "merit" he inspires among the existing shareholders. In 2015, the company had three main shareholders: Elmar Mock (30%); his first partner, Marcel Aeschlimann (28%); and his second partner, André Klopfenstein (20%). These percentages will evolve in the near future, as the company is preparing to pass the torch on to the next generation.

The Salaries

The fixed salaries are lower than at most companies elsewhere on the market and are less than what the colleagues of Creaholic would be able to find in other companies with their qualifications. During a period of recession, with sub-activity, this principle of low basic salaries allowed Creaholic to maintain all of its jobs. During successful years, a variable share of profit may be allocated. This profit sharing of annual benefits is carried out according to an allocation of roughly a third to the partners and two-thirds to the shareholders. Key players of innovation can be designated every year. Choices are made following group discussions about everyone's contribution to the company and how much time was spent on the various projects. In terms of management control, the monitoring of work hours is very accurate: The company knows in real time the turnover of each partner. All of this information is accessible to everyone on the computer network. And so it is not the hierarchy (which does not actually *de facto* exist) who influences the result but rather the shareholder community who shares the majority rule.

The Organization of the Workspace

The company is not structured into departments but is a huge open space divided into three different zones of activity:

- Units or platforms where teams can work on projects together.
- Spaces where people can work or exchange without being involved in any particular project. These areas can be divided into two zones: On the one hand, you have meeting rooms, and on the other hand, you have spaces that are less formal, such as an area for relaxation and a coffee bar. The employees often eat together at the coffee bar, and, once a week, in turn, even the "most experienced" partners have to organize the best possible meal at a minimum cost for everyone.
- Experimental zones for testing and for rapid learning, areas that look similar to test laboratories with 3D printers, laser cutters, metal machining tools, injection machines, and a joinery. This demonstrates the main strength of an Innovation Factory, which is the capacity to experiment rapidly and frequently. Finding the shortest path with the least cost from the concept to reality. No technical staff is designated to these areas: Partners/shareholders use them. It is the consequence of a lack of hierarchy (on one side you have the bosses and on the other side the doers) and the necessity to integrate manual labor with intellectual activity. All movement between the different zones is free and they are very close to one another. This is the price that has to be paid for the company to be agile in the sense that it facilitates movement and intellectual and physical rapidity.

5.5 The Matriarch as a Metaphor of the Management of Ambidexterity

Well-informed companies make the most of their resources in a long-lasting way, enabling them to take full advantage of their offers of products and services. They also have to prepare the future generation of products by innovating. We take the liberty of making a parallel here between industry and wildlife. The matriarch is the mother who will accompany the development of her children. She will bring her babies to maturity. A matriarch does not seek to multiply her children *ad infinitum* but aims to secure the birth rate, hoping to guarantee the survival of the species while making sure that her reproduction efforts are compatible with the educational efforts of the children who are already born. Innovation is to industry what the birth rate is to living organisms. It is vital to avoid confusing the copulation frequency rate with that of the birth rate . . . innovation is the birth rate and creativity is the proposing of new ideas. You can multiply the number of creative seminars and engender a huge amount of breakthrough concepts without actually starting an innovation. How do you end up with innovation? What are the organizational structures and strategies possible for breakthrough innovation? How do you go about reconciling innovation with renovation?

Survival and Conservation

The mother is always in conflict over her short-term survival instinct and her long-term conservation instinct. We know that lions can kill their offspring when they no longer have enough to eat. Survival and conservation do not have the same priorities and do not pertain to the same period of time, but the mother has to take on the responsibility of both simultaneously. In a world that moves fast and frequently, looking out for next week is not enough in order to survive. It is necessary to both live and eat every day and to prepare for future generations. You must hunt and self-reproduce, you have to exploit and to explore. This tension is a well-known fact in innovation management and is referred to as "ambidexterity" (Table 5-1).

A lot of companies have searched and continue to search for ways to innovate for themselves.

To develop inside the company, two conditions have to be combined. First of all, innovation has to start with the desire of the mother. If the mother "does not want to," nothing will happen. If the top management of the company does not want innovation and does not stand by it, apart from an occasional encouraging speech now and again, nothing will be born of it. The mother takes responsibility for bearing the child and also has the right to abort, to stop the process, to kill the innovation budget, for example. The second condition is the capacity to innovate: It is necessary to have an entity or a dedicated organization that makes the activity of innovation possible.

Table 5-1 Ambidexterity—When the Organization Exploits and Explores Simultaneously

The science of the organization has already assimilated the ambivalence that consists of making a set of antagonistic dialectics listen to reason. Ambidexterity shows the way an organization can articulate the activity of daily business with innovation. In this management of ambivalence, the perspective is two-sided: You must make the most of differences (you take from one to help the other), and you must prevent disturbance (from one to the other). Peter Drucker (1974) was one of the first to insist on the impossibility for an organization to manage the existing and to engender novelty. All publications using the term "exploration" refer to the text of the founder James G. March (1991). This explorer of management has defined exploration, which experiments, new and uncertain alternatives, in tension with the exploitation, which perfects and broadens what already exists. According to March, exploration *"includes things (sic) that are understood in terms such as research, variation, risk-taking, experimentation, playing, flexibility, discovery, innovation."* Nowadays, the authors in the management world have pushed the case for a "specialization in" (it is even allowed to say "a differentiation with") the activities of exploration and exploitation. Three forms of organization are described in the literature:

- *Structural ambidexterity*, wherein the activities of exploration and exploitation are distributed among different projects in the same organization that, therefore, manages different projects that are more or less exploratory on a more or less long term
- *Contextual ambidexterity*, wherein the activities of exploration and exploitation are distributed to different projects of the same organization that manages all of the more or less exploratory projects on *a more or less long-term basis*
- *Network ambidexterity*, which separates the exploitation and exploration activities into different legal entities, relevant to different organizations, complementary and articulated

---

Strategies for Breakthrough Innovation and How to Organize It

The metaphor of the matriarch helps show how the Innovation Factory can deal with the current daily business thanks to three kinds of organization that revisit classic ambidexterity (Brion et al., 2008). The point of view we adopt is that of a company which simultaneously exploits and explores and which questions itself about its strategy of breakthrough innovation. And so this company can easily imagine working within an innovative environment rather than simply making innovation itself.

Our Home Nest

This is where the company empowers the breakthrough innovation activity. This is a case of structural ambidexterity. The organization physically separates itself from the rest of the current affairs. The gas separates itself from the crystalline. This "**intra**cubation" presents two major risks: The first is the inclination of the innovation part of the organization to kill the innovation; the second is the tendency to present a clone of the mother rather than a new child. To reassure the company management without any true innovation strategy, it is better for the innovation teams to present it with a replica, with a new version of a known offer rather than risk creating a surprise and being consequently punished for being so bold. You do not go chasing rainbows. Let us go back and take a close look at the first risk, when exploitation catches up with exploration. The new child is a disturbance and transforms its mother. The child to be born is (also) an alien for the mother, causing her to be out of shape and changing her. The body of the mother can also reject the child, considered to be too different from her own organism. A subtle balance has to be set up between the attacks of the organism against the intruder and the antibodies that protect it. In innovation management, you have to protect the exploratory entity from the logical exploitation entity. Indeed, it is always tempting for the company to make exploitation prevail over exploration. If management has to choose between earning short term or taking a risk long term, the choice is quickly made. . . . Safeguarding from internal isolation is ensured by a physical or geographical separation (e.g., a separate design area) and by its own governance principles of exploration that guarantee that it will not be managed like an activity of exploitation (Lenfle, 2008). In relation to this second point, we will underline the importance of finding market-value tools, traditional performance indicators [Key Performance Indicators (KPIs)] in order to avoid killing the innovation in the embryo! A priori innovation is not profitable. It can even transform the way of defining value. It is vital to move the focal point of the evaluation in order to protect, at least for a while, the exploration. What is the added value for the final user in terms of improvement of this practice? What is original, attractive, and desirable in what is explored? Is it reliable and robust, attractive and comfortable? Nobody knew how to define value (and thus the price) of the steam engine before James Watt and Matthew Boulton invented it and commercialized it at the end of the 18th century.

Adoption

In this case, the child is not born of a mother. The child already exists. From the matriarch's point of view, it was developed in vitro before being adopted. The strategy of adoption does not require the need to bear the child. In this case, hunting is your daily business and you adopt for the future. For example, the corporate ventures of big groups (Garel and Jumel, 2005) encourage the acquisition and surveillance of the innovation start-ups. The cost of acquisition can reach incredible heights if it actualizes some of the future benefits. At the same time, the failure rate of this strategy is very high. Some sectors, such as chemistry and pharmaceuticals, are in favor of this strategy, just as certain geographical zones, following the example of Silicon Valley, in California (USA), concentrate huge financial means in risk capital and in numerous innovation start-ups. A start-up is a motherless baby. The start-up is not at risk of being attacked by the internal organisms since it is oriented towards the development of a new activity (in other words, there is no enemy on the inside), but its own environment is hostile and threatens its very existence. To develop and be successful, it has to be adopted by a matriarch, but not too early on and by one who has a few assets and is of a critical size. The dream of the start-up is either to survive alone in its environment or to be adopted by a matriarch-elephant who knows how to cross the desert, finding water at each stop. Mowgli (of the Jungle Book) knows how to cross the jungle alone.

The Nest Elsewhere

This strategy consists of externalizing the breakthrough innovation, outsourcing to an innovation expert, to a breakthrough innovation company. This strategy allows the matriarch to work with external resources in order to develop the "products" different from one's owns and from those that the mother would have made on her own, but which will be finally recognized as hers when they come into existence. This is a strategy of both an external and internal fertilization, it is an Innovation Factory "inside outside" or a co-conception. Creaholic is not a matriarch, but rather a male differentiator, a genetic contributor, an accelerator, even a transformer of the growth of the embryo for its company's clients. These companies entrust Creaholic with a breakthrough task based on a very conceptual and exploratory technical brief or an innovative technological challenge.

Every time, the mandate of the innovation subject is redefined, discussed, adjusted, amended, and co-designed with the client. Incidentally, it is because the mother is a part of the conception from the very beginning that it is more likely she will accept a different daughter from herself. The final cultural shock is not so dramatic, as she is present during all the stages of the design. Any success of the innovation will belong to the mother. It is the company with its brand that will claim the success of the innovation, and it is that company which will diffuse it. This means a good deal of self-effacing and humility is necessary, which can be quite difficult for some creative people who always want to sign their invention and the ensuing innovation. The "Creaholic inside" is a discreet and efficient value for clients B to B but not a brand for the final client. The teams involved on the outside are only present for the insemination and pre-educational period. Like birds that make their nests, they fertilize and accompany the beginning of the growth of the newborn. The next stage in the growth is the responsibility of the client. The breakthrough innovation company contributed some of its genetics in order to create innovation. It did not get involved in the exploitation and can, therefore, preserve its agility and be ready to multifertilize.

5.6 Multidisciplinary and Multifertilization

Clients come to a breakthrough innovation company for its ability to multifertilize. It is essential not to confuse multidisciplinarity and multifertilization. Multidisciplinarity is an exchange between representatives of different disciplines concerning a particular subject. Each discipline maintains its method of explanation and is not transformed by this interaction. The juxtaposition of the disciplinary perspectives opens up the sphere of knowledge (no more K base), but here the engineer remains an engineer and the designer (for example) a creative person. Everybody stays focused on discipline. This type of coordination, which makes good use of the interdisciplinary qualities of the specialists, is efficient in the case of stable frameworks and rule-based design strategies or of renovation. Multifertilization, on the other hand, transforms the knowledge of those who are involved. It goes further than just the juxtaposition of disciplines. Because it happens when you have to face up to new questions, it opens up new perspectives for established know-how, violently shaking them up. The experts stumble together over unknown, unstable, and exploratory questions. When electronics engineers along with other experts first move into the food sector they remain electronics engineers, but they address new issues because they are now in an unfamiliar work environment. Furthermore, if the electronics engineers have already been in the field of varied exploration, they are potentially multifertile inseminators. "For our clients, we do not belong to their field of expertise; we have already discovered other domains of expertise and that is what is of interest to them in order to achieve their innovation!" explain the managers of Creaholic. The bee uses different types of pollen, and it is the fruit that interests the client. The violin from Vienna sounds different from the Cajun one, and yet it is the same instrument. But the territories, the stories, and the different cultures that have created the same product have two different uses for it, and two different types of sounds that are created with it. Because these teams have worked in many different kinds of environments, Creaholic knows how to play with both of the violins for its clients, who are respected specialists of one single instrument in one particular culture. In Table 5-2, it is the width of the T that illustrates the

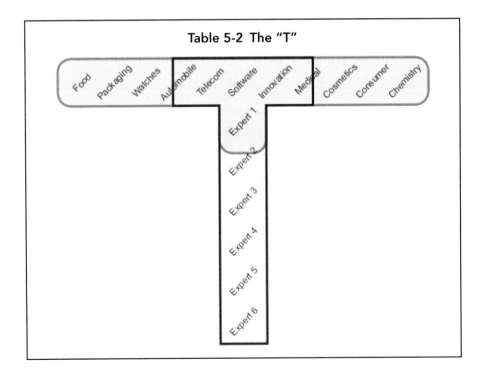

Table 5-2 The "T"

extent of the knowledge (a wide K base), and its depth that symbolizes the specialization of the necessary knowledge for the exploitation.

When multifertilization is required, the Innovation Factory outsources (width of the K's) when the internal resources are not sufficient in order to produce (depth of the K's). *"Our clients are specialists; we offer them the huge scope of our expertise and the reassurance that we will not compete against them,"* sums up the managers of Creaholic.

Of course, there are other organizations and innovation strategies that reconcile the constraints of ambidexterity. We have neither talked about the role of national public authorities nor the numerous territorial ecosystems of innovation that knit together the private/public strategies. The notion of open innovation is still flying high, even if it is tautological—there is no closed innovation process! Open innovation kicks into action in physical spaces of collaborative and open design (third parties, fablabs, hackerspaces, techshops, etc.) as well as on virtual platforms, more or less owned or open and more or less modular. This state of affairs addresses issues such as financing, creativity, and problem solving. "The" perfect innovation organization does not exist. Only good rules of organization exist. Let us retain two of them at the end of this chapter. First, it is not the same organization that has to deal with the exploitation and the exploration. And second, the right organization is not necessarily internal. The Innovation Factory needs to have a network of relations with breakthrough environments for all companies who are trapped within their own specializations.

Epilogue

Watches to be Watched: Connected Watches, or the Innovation War Raging on Your Wrist

And what comes next? Breakthrough innovation is not a subject for any epilogue, as it continues to make the horizon of "what is known" recede while the future is reinvented. . . . At this final stage of the book, let us go back to the theme of watchmaking and ask ourselves: What are the new issues that are taking this established sector by assault? What is happening here and now to watchmakers? What has to be designed in watchmaking today? What are the new horizons? We have to stop confusing the watch with the watch-making industry. The watch is the object that you wear on your wrist, whereas watchmaking is the sector that has been designing, making, and selling this object for a very long period of time. At the beginning of the 21st century, the equivalent of the pocket watch was the portable telephone. What we will be wearing on our wrist tomorrow is a new oxymoron: a watch is no longer a watch—it is a connected watch. The best way to innovate in the watchmaking industry is to . . . make a watch, another kind of watch, one that will certainly draw into its design arena new and highly successful companies.

The longevity of the Swatch is a true success, but the little watch is now on the decline. In general, the innovation game of watchmaking is being played elsewhere and differently, with other key players who are unfamiliar with watchmaking tradition and with Switzerland. Their names are Samsung and Apple, but there are many others—Sony, Lenovo, Garmin, or LG—who belong to the community of the first big companies to launch connected watches, thereby "disrupting" the watchmaking industry. Watchmaking has reinvented itself many times in the past, from the nomadic object that tells the time, to the fashion item, to the object you might be lucky to inherit. Communication with objects is increasing in a dramatic manner. Some sources reckon that roughly 50 billion objects will be connected all over the world in 2020 for a market of more than US$7,000 billion. Ethical and environmental debate is well under way. In this trend of connected objects, the watch is one of the most emblematic of all. A connected watch is a high-technology object that is worn on your wrist and identified by an IP address. It gives you multiple applications that connect you to your watch, other individuals, and a non-human environment. If the first "intelligent watches" already appeared on the scene back in the early 1980s, they were only capable of doing simple tasks, such as sums or the management of a simple agenda. Connected watches started to really emerge at the beginning of 2010, and so it is hard to have any real perspective on the subject at present. According to a recent study conducted by Statista, 6.8 million connected watches were sold all over the world in 2014. That same year, Switzerland sold 28.6 million complete watches in a global market of roughly 1.2 billion pieces. Are we witnessing the birth of a new kind of market? Is this merely an ephemeral gadget? As with all beginnings of any distribution of an innovation, what exists already has a tendency to resist and does not know how to judge this novelty. Connected watches are taking a battering, especially concerning their usefulness.* Our intention is not to cling onto a topical subject. We merely want to examine it by taking a step back from what is at stake and from the new functions that this object offers. We take the start of this story of the connected watch very seriously.

---

* Let us not forget that in France, a few years before the cell phone became a huge success, people who were interviewed said there was no market for them: *"No, I don't need a portable telephone; I already have a Bi-Bop; there are telephone boxes everywhere; I am not a doctor and don't have a job that requires for me to be contactable at all times . . ."*

From a Coordinated World to a Connected World

Before time was measured it was observed. During the summer seasons, people worked longer hours as the day was longer. For many centuries, time was told by the shadow cast by a gnomon. It was the cycles of the day and night, of seasons and the stars, that defined "natural" time. As long as astrology and astronomy were intertwined in the calendars, and as long the same man defined both when to ring the hours and when to say the prayers, then time continued to testify to a divine presence. Progressively, scientific time would replace the time of God. The bells and the sundials were replaced by the clocks on the steeples of the churches of the Dark Ages. In the 17th century, in the footsteps of Copernicus, Galileo upheld a mechanistic definition of time and of its calculation, a physical time. This new time adapted itself to science and to trade. It enabled merchant activity to be coordinated in a world that was already internationalized. Time became portable, movable, even at sea. Watchmaking techniques progressed and gained in precision. The triumphant era of capitalism in the 20th century forced men and women to coordinate together on a huge scale in order to work, catch the train, meet up, synchronize machines, etc.

The watch has always been a connected object; time for oneself makes no sense. The notion of connection is consubstantial to watchmaking and is not new. However, the nature and the extent of this contemporary connection is different and makes us distinguish between coordination and connection. When the company Nokia started its metamorphosis in the telecom industry at the beginning of the 1990s, the company launched a brilliant new slogan: "*Connecting people.*" This phrase announced the extension and the acceleration of the connection: connection to oneself, to objects, to others, to the flux of continuous information in the private and in the public world. This surpassed the basic knowledge of the individual (I know and somebody else also knows), but it also went further than any collective knowledge (everybody knows). What has been produced is what the sociologists and the IT specialists call "global knowledge" (everybody knows that everybody else knows). It is under this condition that we can work together in a peer-to-peer relation connected by the network. The marketplace of the village has become gigantic. Moreover, this connection is mobile and adds to the increasing speed of our society (Hartmut, 2010): The flux of information comes to us all the time everywhere. In a connected and digital world, the mastery of the watchmaking mechanical complexity no longer makes any sense in relation to the world mass market. Incidentally, the Swiss watch bosses owe their economic salvation to the market niche of luxury watches. We are not multi-wristed Shivas; we will not wear two watches on the same wrist, a traditional one and a connected one. Today's young Westerners do not have to wear a watch to know what time it is. The watch was developed at the same time as the calendar. Today, the telephone, the watch, and the calendar are all interconnected, allowing individuals to find one another without any precise preliminary coordination concerning the time and the place. A *rendezvous* is finalized by a little bit of last minute coordination: *"I am here now and who from my tribe wants to come and find me?"* This competition is now influencing the redefining of what we will wear on our wrists.

The Economic War on Your Wrist

Some big companies have completely changed the telecom landscape by designing the smartphone. The same people are now handling the wrist. An economic battle is raging. The leaders of high-tech for all have caused an upheaval and conquered the market of the mobile telephone in less than ten years and are currently searching for new growth levers. For these firms, who have astronomical financial means, the connected watch is an obvious choice: It is small and portable, and the margins are high. It is also capable of mastering big data algorithms, platforms of content, and exploitation systems (such as Android Wear of Google). It is a major venture of the Internet of objects. The system control that exploits the new connected devices ensures the economic control of potentially massive markets: health, medical, telecommunications, domotics, payments, leisure activities, etc.

And what about Switzerland? Every year, Switzerland ranks high among the most innovative countries in the world. All the necessary knowledge for the development of an intelligent watch can be found in the Jura Arc area: the display technology, the miniature captors, the low-consumption cordless communications, or the managing of energy, with or without a battery. Just think about the technology that is mastered by the CSEM (*Centre suisse d'électronique et de microtechnique*). However, Silicon Valley was the first to create a buzz about connected watches. Is history repeating itself again? In Chapter 2, we have recounted the story of the crisis of the 1970s and its effects on the Swiss watchmaking industry.

We saw how the barons of the field were convinced that the crisis would only be temporary and that Switzerland would survive the awful Asian attacks. Today, it is obvious that the very big computer companies as well as those specialized in content and telephony will produce massive amounts of watches. The Swiss watchmaking industry could have taken the initiative. Apple had approached Swatch . . . but they declined the offer. Once the blow had been delivered by these new competitors in the watchmaking market, the Swiss should have reacted immediately: They should have dealt their cards making the most of their historical advance and their mastery of luxury.[*]

Some watchmaking bosses were first indifferent, reticent,[†] lacking in interest, before changing their minds, one after the other, in 2015, once the Apple Watch was revealed to the general public. TAG Heuer has developed a model in partnership with Intel and Google. Guess, Breitling, and Swatch have launched their own connected watches in 2015. What can we learn of importance from this reinvention of the watch and . . . from watchmaking?

The Wrist: An Innovative Spot[‡]

The watch we wear on our wrist is a product of recent history. Up until the end of WWI, it was the pocket watch that was in every gentleman's waistcoat. The wristwatch was, first of all, a piece of jewelry for women

---

[*] As long as the connected watch stays on the wrist, it remains a watch that comes within the scope of watchmaking semiology: The watch is also a talisman, a social symbol, a means of expressing one's fears and one's beliefs. It represents a lifestyle. Because extremely expensive products with very innovative designs are being made for it, the connected watch sees its symbolic, ostentatious, and imaginary side that it already possesses increased. The story continues in the same way: You do not buy a Cartier watch to read the time; you do not buy a $20,000 Apple Watch in rose gold to read your SMS's.

[†] Before thinking better of it, the boss and owner of the Swatch Group, Nick Hayek, warned that his group *did not have a calling for the launching of a portable telephone attached to the wrist.*

[‡] Let us think back to 1974 when Roland Moreno, the inventor of the smart card, filed a patent application for a ring. He does not yet know how he will use his invention, but this location opens up the space for many applications.

before turning into a military item at the turn of the 20th century (it was necessary to read time outside, in all circumstances, despite one's gear). And thereafter, many a wristwatch was used in all sorts of everyday situations while certain brands surrounded them in mystery, creating a form of mythology (the abyssal depths, aviation, sports). The connected watch makes the most of this particular spot on the human body.

Palmistry believes that the wrist is a zone of luck, and traditional jewelers know to what extent it occupies a place of charm and seduction. The wrist is above all, one of those most sensitive areas of the human body, combining numerous nerve ends and is visually very accessible. It facilitates self-communication. There are technologies that exploit this sensitive situation. The connected watch is proprioceptive, which means that it is sensitive to the perception of the positioning of the body in a physical space. On the other hand tri-dimensional captors transmit vibrations to the wrist. The watch becomes a blind man's cane, a manual system of orientation, an electronic station of movement control. The corporal contact with the connected watch heralds the development of health applications already being developed on the smartphones. Am I good-looking? Am I in good health? Reinsurance becomes a permanent thing. . . . The watches can overcome the hurdle that the phones are stumbling on: physiology. Demands are no longer made on the screen but rather on the captors behind the device and on the bracelet; both are in contact with the skin. The body is observed and analyzed (pulse, physical activity); soon, the barrier of the epidermis will be crossed, making possible blood tests, eye testing, and the taking of one's temperature. . . .

The connected world relies much more than the coordinated world on information. The continual assault of data produces such a wealth of facts that a few principles and a certain amount of pertinent filtering systems are required: What is relevant to me among the overwhelmingly abundant information? What have I missed? What can I postpone? What needs to be looked at urgently? What is important? The connected watch automatically processes the information. Instead of looking at your phone 200 times a day, the watch sends signals (indications on the screen or vibrations) that sort out the information (including advertizing . . .) This is a new form of good manners, we are more dicreet when we read our messages. I do not need to look at my watch any more since it sends me a signal. I speak to someone and the watch listens to me and decides whether to disturb me (or not) according to the degree of urgency. The connected watch frees the eye from the stress of screens and reintroduces discretion into our society.

Watchmaking Seized by a Revolution

The connected watch does not mean we are witnessing the end of the portable phone any more than the Kalachnikov made the Samorai's sword disappear. On the other hand, new relationships are being built between the two apparatuses, in a relationship based on a sort of dependency. The watch is not intended to reproduce the functions of the smartphone. It certainly does not aspire to become a system as intelligent as the telephone. The watch will be a slave to the smartphone, dependent on a system more intelligent and more complete than itself, providing a softer and simplified usage. The watch relays the phone with elementary functions during a jog, for example, and also adds a few more appropriate sports applications. The watch temporarily replaces the telephone in situations where it is too risky to take it along. The watch's safety is pretty basic, as it is attached to the wrist: The risks of loss or theft are not as high as with a telephone.

Connected watches are evolutionary. They will develop based on the applications that their clients will design and adopt. The object is reinventing itself, regenerating itself, and changing the definition of its durability. We go from generational durability to generative goods with new uses. The connected watch will evolve with its new applications and should not normally be thrown away at each new innovation. The innovation will emanate from the applications, but the "cockpit" that will take care of them will be more sustainable than the renewal cycle of the contents. Watchmaking has switched from the mastering of mechanical cogs to the adeptness of electronics and algorithms. The connected watch massively opens up the "K" base of design. The new generation of creative watchmakers will bring together mathematicians, electronics engineers, micro-mechanical engineers, designers, and marketing specialists, as well as the makers because you have to test, DIY, and prototype rapidly and often. From the traditional watchmaking point of view, it is a new generation of innovators who need to be trained and associated to new ecosystems. The arrival of social networks and this state of permanent connection has caused an upheaval in the positioning of brands, distribution channels, and design. The creative power of the masses, the creative autonomy of ordinary people is a celebration of the invention of the "profane professionals." These products will adapt themselves even better to our multiple and personal needs because their countless applications are being designed by "people like us" in communities (Cohendet, Llerena, and Simon, 2010; Chanal and Caron-Fasan, 2010).

These upheavals are taking place right now as we are writing this book. One of the main precepts learned from breakthrough design is that it allows you to review known identities about the objects that surround us. The challenge for watchmaking will be to define new uses and new appropriations. The results of the good innovation factories are quite surprising and more than satisfactory. The watch went from the pocket to the wrist. It is now reinventing itself on the wrist. Who knows? It might even end up in our clothes or on other parts of the human body. Inventors are taking the time to think about the watch as are the watchmakers and many others.

Conclusion

Innovation at Work

If innovation is both a result of the act of innovation and of the action itself, our book positions itself from the point of view of the process. Innovation is a specific activity with certain clear-cut characteristics that set it apart and yet confront it with other forms of activity that can also be managed, like production or decision. All the chapters in this book underline the fact that these specific activities are made according to their own set of rules.[*] And so, how do you create innovation? What are the forms of governance that make or impede it? Traditional approaches of the management of innovation have answered these questions (see Table C-1).

All of these approaches are influenced by two trends in the management of conception: the rule-based mode and the innovative mode (Le Masson, Weil, and Hatchuel, 2007). You either renovate or you go out and make a revolution; you either stay in incremental innovation or you take the risk of making radical innovation; you either revise the identity of the objects or you persist in the parametric conception of the established dominant design.[†] Even though there are two different design methods for innovation, it is not about pitting them against each other, based on

---

[*] For the question, "Can you manage innovation?," see http://media.cnam.fr/peut-on-gerer-l-innovation-470355.kjsp.

[†] You play with the known parameters of known identities of known objects: smaller, cheaper, quicker, lighter.

Table C-1 How Do You Innovate? Traditional Approaches of the Management of Innovation

An individual, singular exploit, unrepeatable
An exploit of a certain category of actors, of a job, a profession—the engineers, the marketing specialists, the designers . . .
Have good ideas, have original ideas, be creative
Gather a great amount of competencies, instruct, and decide
Trial and error approach
Science, techniques, applications: fundamental research/applied research
Investment in R&D
Answer to needs and expectations
Attractive public politics
Entrepreneurship, intrapreneurship
Project management
Corporate venturing, sprinkling, acquisition, incubation

value judgments (such as "It would be better to be more innovative than rule-based"), but it is more about finding out how you can do both at the same time.

In truth, the principles of the management of rule-based design do not allow breakthrough innovation to happen. In order to make breakthrough innovation, you must reconcile concept with knowledge. The *Cirque du Soleil* has revolutionized the circus world and has as many engineers as artists working for them to create the dream that we are sold. The same is true of the Swatch, which needed to have as many "creative" engineers as "engineering" designers on board for it to see the light of day. That is why we have tried to avoid certain clichés concerning innovation, which only reduce the factory to a simple creative feat or to a certain amount of knowledge. Indeed, there are not only "creative people" on the concept side and "erudite people" on the knowledge side. With the C-K Theory of the *Centre de recherche en gestion des MINES ParisTech*, we have been able to distinguish between concept and knowledge while simultaneously explaining how they are both articulated around the design approach. The concepts are those attractive "unknowns" that allow us to go past the frame of mind of "assert what you want to prove." By formulating a concept, we allow ourselves the chance to imagine and even to dream. Knowledge is always anchored in principles of proof and facts that are defined as logical proposals. There is no longer a need to be different in order to be innovative (phew!), and it is no longer necessary to be (only) a "wise man." The C-K breakthrough innovation design approach "forces" the concepts to spread, clarifying their definitions thanks to knowledge. Vice versa, new concepts lead to the acquisition of new knowledge or the capacity to design them. With the Swatch, we saw how a knowledge of plastics processing was useless without the concept of the cheap innovative watch, and, in turn, the concept forced the knowledge to spread from the plastics to marketing and design. The conditions for the reconciliation of concept with knowledge are complex but they can be controlled. It is important to make something very clear: It is not because an innovation process is controllable that it is predictable! No organization will ever be sure *ex ante* that it can achieve radical innovation. It will never reach its goals if it does not reconcile concept with knowledge. This is the role of the liquid mental state (Chapter 4), which must preserve this space and essential for the exchange between concept and knowledge.

When you produce radical innovation you have to favor action, which means going from a logic of preparation, planning, and anticipating to a "logic of action." Basically, the latter is linked to scripting, prototyping, trials, experimentation, in a nutshell, all the forms of moving into action. You have to do to find out. We saw it with the "*Schnaps-Idee*," the barroom idea of the Swatch, with that very first drawing of the future watch; if that simple sketch was able to speak to Ernst Thomke, it was because he possessed a certain know-how of micro-technical watchmaking, and, therefore, he knew how to read it. And because he already had an idea at the back of his mind about the concept of the watch, he was able to imagine the huge potential of the drawing. For those who innovate, it is necessary to have a representation "that speaks" of the object to be designed: a drawing, a model, a physical or virtual prototype. . . . The representations of the objects fulfill essential functions in an Innovation Factory, for they represent what does not (yet) exist, formalizing and confronting the representations, helping to validate, learn about the process in advance, learn to control, test, or to simulate it. The use of physical objects is a privileged mode of representation of the object to be. The use of such objects by designers leads to a mutual exchange of what is explicit and what is "tacit," in the same manner as a music teacher who plays a note on his instrument showing his pupil what he expects of him. Knowledge or concept must express itself, it must exist socially, it has to be formalized and not remain confined to the slightly symbolic world of its owners. "We have in mind the idea of a revolutionary watch! Very good, show us what you are capable of." What we know is not only expressed in words but also figuratively; drawings are sketched, photos taken, noises made, blobs of play-doh or other materials are used for rapid assembling. Quick prototypes and virtual reality are both used. In other words, physical objects support and facilitate the representation of "what we have in mind." They allow us to help others understand by making them listen, by making them feel. The scholar Ikujiro Nonaka (1994) defines "externalization" as a process that transforms tacit knowledge (I can know how to do something and yet not know how to explain what I know, nor how I do it) into explicit knowledge. Innovation activity demands all sorts of rapid expressions; the activity of breakthrough innovative design favors direct contact in the field and practice. We know how pointless it is to question the client about radical innovation because he does not even know what he wants. Refraining from asking your clients does not mean that you kill the concept. "I have no idea of what I want but I will tell you when I see it" (Thomke and Bell, 2001). "That is exactly what I asked you to develop but it is not what I wanted" (Thomke, 2001).

Faced with disturbing concepts and disconcerting promises of radical innovation the influential managers must not cogitate too long, nor think of the potential risks. You have to go against the trend of a lot of "directors" of "opening up the umbrella," who request a financial analysis before backing an innovation. We saw this with the example of the distribution of the watch Swatch: E. Thomke and ETA had "tried everything" without any preconceptions. Since the Swiss watch retailers did not want to sell the plastic watch, the company turned to department stores, sports shops, and large discount stores. . . . A priori judgments blocked the innovation activity. When there is no precise target, as with a development project, with a brief, the objective is constructed progressively with the learning process. In the activity of radical innovation, the move to action is favored because we do not really know where we are going; everything is tried and adjustments are made. We do it either in a parallel fashion, sequentially, or by trying to combine the two. Everything is good! The same applies to the learning process—everything is relevant: working undercover, experimentation, acquisition, training, sharing, research. . . .

We have described the rules that govern Creaholic, a breakthrough innovation company, created by a gaseous individual who was frustrated with the crystalline state, whose team of multidisciplinary experts have imagined and found new ways of design for their clients and for themselves for more than thirty years. Indeed, it is possible to repeat innovation over and over again! Nurture the pearls you possess by knowing how to find their disturbing factors, identify the disjunctions between knowledge and concept, maintain a mental state of ebullition, exchange with the crystals in order to go from exploration to exploitation to master, acquire, and conceive knowledge. The path towards innovation is complex and not without risk, but never give up! We hope that this book proves that breakthrough innovation is an art that can be mastered.

References

Amabile, T. M. *Creativity in Context: Update to the Social Psychology of Creativity.* Boulder: Westview Press, 1996.

Argyris, C. and Schön, D. A. *Apprentissage organisationnel. Théorie, méthode, pratique.* DeBoeck Université, 1996.

Benghozi, P. J., Charue-Duboc, F., and Midler, C. *Innovation Based Competition & Design Systems Dynamics.* L'Harmattan, 2000.

Brion, S., Fabre-Bonte, V., and Mothe, C. "Quelles formes d'ambidextrie pour combiner innovations d'exploitation et d'exploration?" *Management International* 13, no. 3 (2008).

Carrera, R. *Swatchissimo, l'extraordinaire aventure de la Swatch.* Antiquorum Éditions, 1991.

Chanal, V. and Caron-Fasan, M. L. "The Difficulties Involved in Developing Business Models Opened to Innovation Communities: The Case of a Crowdsourcing Platform." *M@n@gement* 13, no. 4 (2010): 318–341.

Chapel, V. "Tefal: un modèle de croissance intensive." *Entreprises et Histoire* 23 (1999): 63–76.

Chesbrough, H. W. "The Era of Open Innovation." *Sloan Management Review* 44, no. 3 (2003): 35–41.

Choulier, D. *Comprendre l'activité de conception.* Université Technologie Belfort Montbéliard, 2009.

Choulier, D., Forest, J., and Coatanéa, E. "The C-K Engineering Design Theory: Contributions and Limits." Proceedings of the 22nd International Conference on Design Theory and Methodology, Montréal, Québec, August 15–18, 2010.

Christensen, C. *The Innovator's Dilemma.* Harvard Business School Press, 1997.

Cohendet, P., Llerena, P., and Simon, L. "The Innovative Firm: Nexus of Communities and Creativity." *Revue d'Economie Industrielle* 129–130 (2010): 139–170.

Danesi, M. "Marques suisses, Swatch: Le mythe des origines." *Domaine Public* 27 (mai 2005). Accessed from http://www.domainepublic.ch/articles/1217.

David, A. "Décision, conception et recherche en sciences de gestion." *Revue française de gestion* 3, no. 139 (2002): 173–185.

Donzé, P. Y. *Histoire de l'industrie horlogère suisse. De Jacques David à Nicolas Hayek (1850–2000).* Neuchâtel: Éd. Alphil, 2009.

Drucker, P. *Management: Tasks, Responsibilities, Practices.* New York, NY: Harper & Row, 1974.

Duncan, J. and Fitzpatrick, L. *Avatar.* Éditions de l'Archipel, 2010.

Ellul, J. *La Technique ou l'enjeu du siècle.* Economica, 1990.

Elmquist, M. and Segrestin, B. "The Challenges of Managing Open Innovation in Highly Innovative Fields: Exploring The Use of the KCP Method." Euram conference, Track: 14. Innovation—Continuing the Journey, Liverpool, 2009.

Fiell, C. and Fiell, P. *Design Industrial.* Taschen, 2006.

Gabarro, J. and Zehnder, D. "Nicolas G. Hayek." Harvard Business School case, June 17, 1994, 9-495-005.

Garel, G. and Jumel, S. "Les grands groupes et l'innovation: définitions et enjeux du corporate venture." *Finance Contrôle Stratégie* 8, no. 4 (déc 2005): 33–61,.

Garel, G. and Crottet, D. "Innover ou gaspiller, la révolution simple du lavage des mains." *Impertinence*, La Documentation Française, 2011, 105–114.

Godelier, E. "Est-ce que vous avez un garage? Ou discussions d'un mythe international de la culture managériale." In *Le Meilleur de la stratégie et du management*, edited by Benghozi, P. J. and Huet, J. M., 74–77. Pearson, 2009.

Hargadon, A. "Knowledge Brokering: A Network Perspective on Learning and Innovation." In *Research in Organizational Behavior*, edited by Staw B. and Kramer R. JAI Press, 2002, 21, 41–85.

Hartmut, R. *Accélération? Une critique sociale du temps.* La Découverte, 2010.

Hatchuel, A., Le Masson, P., and Weil, B. "Design Theory and Collective Creativity: A Theoretical Framework to Evaluate KCP Process." XVII International Conference on Engineering Design, Stanford University, 2009.

Hatchuel, A., Le Masson, P., and Weil, B. "C-K Theory in Practice: Lessons from Industrial Applications." 8th International Design Conference, Dubrovnik, May 2004, 245–257.

Hatchuel, A. and Weil, B. "Pour une théorie unifiée de la conception, Axiomatiques et processus collectifs." CGS Ecole des Mines / GIS cognition-CNRS, Paris, 1999, 1–27.

Hatchuel, A. and Weil, B. "La Théorie C-K: fondements et usages d'une théorie unifiée de la conception." Lyon: Colloque Sciences de la Conception, 2002.

Hatchuel, A. and Weil, B. "A New Approach of Innovative Design: An Introduction to C-K Design Theory." ICED'03, Stockholm, Sweden, 2003.

Hayek, N. G. *Au-delà de la saga Swatch—Entretiens d'un authentique entrepreneur avec Bartu Friedemann*. Albin Michel, 2006.

Koller, C. *L'Industrialisation et l'État au pays de l'horlogerie. De la lime à la machine*. Courrendlin: Éditions CJE, 2003.

Komar, D. and Planche, F. *A Guide to: Swatchwatches*. OTWD On Time Diffusion SA, 1995.

Le Bé, P. "Nicolas G. Hayek, de l'énergie pour un siècle." L'Hebdo, 30 juin 2010.

Le Masson, P. *Management de l'innovation et théories de la conception: nouvelles rationalités, nouveaux principes d'organisation, nouvelles croissances*. Habilitation à diriger des recherches, Université Paris Est, 2008.

Le Masson, P., Hatchuel, A., and Weil, B. "Creativity and Design Reasoning: How C-K Theory can enhance creative design." *International Conference on Engineering Design, ICED'07*, Paris, 12, 2007.

Le Masson, P., Weil, B., and Hatchuel, A. *Les Processus d'innovation—Conception innovante et croissance des entreprises*. Hermès, 2006.

Le Masson, P., Weil, B., and Hatchuel, A. *Strategic Management of Design and Innovation*. Cambridge University Press, 2010.

Lenfle, S. "Exploration and Project Management." *International Journal of Project Management* 25, no. 6 (2008): 469–478.

Maniak, R. and Midler, C. "Shifting From Co-development Process to Co-innovation." *International Journal of Automotive and Technology Management* 8, no. 4 (2008): 449–454.

March, J. G. "Exploration and Exploitation in Organizational Learning." *Organization Science* 2, no. 1 (1991): 71–87.

Moon, Y. "The Birth of Swatch." Harvard Business School case, 2004, 0-504-096.

Müller, J. and Mock, E. "Eine Revolution in der Uhrentechnik." *Neuen Zurcher Zeitung*. 2 mars 1983.

Nonaka, I. "A Dynamic Theory of Organizational Knowledge Creation." *Organization Science* 5, no. 1 (February 1994): 14–37.

Oslo Manual. *Guidelines for Collecting and Interpreting Innovation Data*, 3rd ed. 2005, 10.

Pasquier, H. *La "Recherche et Développement" en horlogerie. Acteurs, stratégies et choix technologiques dans l'Arc jurassien suisse (1900–1970)*, Neuchâtel: Alphil, 2008.

Pinson, C. and Kimbal, H. *Swatch, Insead Case Study* 5, 1987.

Simon, H. *Les Sciences de l'artificiel.* Gallimard, 2004.

Taylor, W. "Message and Muscle: An Interview with Swatch Titan Nicolas Hayek." *Harvard Business Review,* March–April 1993, 99–110.

Thomke, S. "Enlightened Experimentation: The New Imperative for Innovation." *Harvard Business Review,* February 2001, 67–75.

Thomke, S. and Bell, D. E. "Sequential Testing in Product Development." *Management Science* 47, no. 2 (February 2001): 308–323.

Trueb, L. *The World of Watches: History, Technology, Industry.* Ebner Publishing International, 2005.

Trueb, L. "Eine Idee aus Plastic erobert die Welt." *Neue Zürcher Zeitung.* 4 avril 2008.

Trueb, L. Discours en l'honneur des lauréats du prix Gaïa 2010, Elmar Mock et Jacques Müller, 16 septembre 2010.

Tushman, M. L. and Radov, D. "The Rebirth of the Swiss Swatch Industry, 1980–1992 (A)." Harvard Business School case, 2000, 9-400-087.

Utterback, J. L. and Abernathy, W. J. "A Dynamic Model of Process and Product Innovation." *Omega, The International Journal of Management Science* 3, no. 6 (1975): 639–656.

Von Hippel, E. "Lead Users: A Source of Novel Product Concepts." *Management Science* 32, no. 7 (July 1986): 791–805.

Wegelin, J. *Mister Swatch: Nicolas Hayek und das Geheimnis seines Erfolges.* Éditions Nagel & Kimche, 2009.

Index